YOUR
PASTOR
NEEDS THIS BOOK

YOUR
PASTOR
NEEDS THIS BOOK

5 HUGE MISTAKES YOU CAN HELP
YOUR
PASTOR AVOID

RJBELL

♠ Four ♠ Bells ♠ Publishing ♠

ISBN 978-0-9857399-0-4   [Softcover]

ISBN 978-0-9857399-1-1   [eBook]

Printed in the United States of America

Table of Contents
★★★★★★★★

A Word from the Author

One of the perils of writing a book of this nature is the danger of being misunderstood and viewed as a prophet of doom and gloom. It would be very easy for the reader of this book to conclude that the writer sees no hope for the problem he is addressing. But if that were the case, it would be folly for me to put ink to paper.

In a court of law there are two sides in the court room. The prosecutor sits on one side and the defense on the other. They both have jobs to do. The prosecutor's job is to take a case and make it look bad, so bad in fact that there is no room for optimism, while the defense's job is take the same case and make it look good. The defense's job is to give cause for optimism. One takes the brush and paints a gloomy, dark picture with no hope; the other takes the brush and paints a beautiful, sunny picture of hope.

As you read the chapters of this book, it will appear that I am painting a picture of hopelessness in our battle against our sinful nature. It will appear thus, because I am magnifying just the fleshly nature of man. I suppose I am playing the prosecutor in the case of man versus lust.

Before I prosecute, let me introduce you to your defender in this struggle of flesh versus spirit, good versus evil.

His Name is Jesus Christ.

His credentials, of which no other man ever born of woman can boast, are nail marks in His hands and feet, a spear scar on His side, and a folded napkin at

A Word From The Author

the head of an empty tomb. As a defender, His sacrificial blood has been applied to every sin imaginable; any black sin, regardless of how fifthly and despicable, that has ever had His blood applied to it, instantly vanished in the sight of the Father.

His record as a defender is impeccable; <u>He has never lost a case</u>. Any person who has ever come to Him in faith, and asked forgiveness, has been forgiven. <u>Jesus Christ is our only hope</u> in our unrelenting battle against our sinful nature hidden in our flesh.

Romans 7:24-25 [NIV]
24 What a wretched man I am! Who will rescue me from this body of death? 25 Thanks be to God—through Jesus Christ our Lord!

****

At this station in my life I have more gray than brown in my hair. I have far more sunsets in my rear view mirror, as opposed to peering through my windshield. These benefits give me a completely different perspective concerning people, especially preachers.

In my youth, as with most ambitious young preachers, I would have probably been very easily offended if you did not agree with the exhortation I was putting forth. But not so today, mostly because of a lesson I learned a long time ago.

The Lesson
Years ago my wife and I attended a seminar for ministers held at a secluded YMCA camp on the eastern side of the Ozark Mountains near Potosi, Missouri. The camp was one of those breathtakingly beautiful places that you visit and wonder, how can I ever leave all the beauty that surrounds me and return to the real world?

YOUR PASTOR NEEDS THIS BOOK

The seminar was to be a laid back event. No suits or ties. No busy schedule. Just a few classes during the day and then time to hang out with friends, play some games, and relax.

I have never forgotten something I learned in one of the classes; it would forever change the way I view people and their opinions.

The instructor had a picture on an easel in the front of the room where we sat. The picture was covered with a bed sheet so no one could see it until the instructor was ready to reveal it.

It was pretty obvious that it was going to be an object lesson.

The instructor handed out pencils and paper. He then told us he was going to remove the sheet and we would see a picture. He told us that we might be able to see hidden objects or forms drawn into the picture. Our assignment was to look at the painting and if we saw any hidden objects in the painting, we were to write down what we saw on our paper. No one other than the instructor would see what we had written on our paper.

The instructor removed the sheet and there resting on the easel was a beautiful painting of a very rugged mountain scene, which I assumed to be the Rocky Mountains. The amazing thing about the picture was that entwined in the rocks and trees of the mountains, I immediately saw a ship. There it was, as bold as the noonday sun--a ship in the mountains. The artist was brilliant; I had never seen anything like it in my life. The instructor told us, "If you see an object in the painting, go to another area of the room and see if the object is visible from another angle." I walked to different locations in the room and was

A Word From The Author

amazed, from any location in the room; I could clearly see 'the ship.'

Our instructor told us to write on our paper any hidden objects we were able to see in the painting, and then pass our paper to him. I proudly wrote 'ship'. He took our papers and began dividing them into two stacks. I felt confused, wondering, why two stacks? I understood one stack, the picture of the ship. But I did not understand the second stack.

Then he asked, "If you see the ship, raise your hand." Several others raised their hands, me among them. Then he asked, "If you see the airplane, raise your hand." Some other people raised their hands. I thought, what airplane? That was the second stack of papers, the airplane. Then he asked for a show of hands from those that saw neither the ship nor the airplane. At that point most of the other hands went up.

Then the fun began. The people who could see the ship or the airplane hidden in the painting were told to find someone seated nearby who could not see the ship or the airplane; <u>we were to help them see the hidden objects we saw</u>.

After all, we are ministers; our job is to help people see things that are hidden from them. Every Sunday we climb up on the pulpit and teach or preach so people can see things in the Bible that they have not been able to see. Furthermore, we expect those in the pews to see what we are preaching or teaching, and we expect those listening to see it exactly as we do. After all, we see it so clearly.

Try to imagine thirty people who could see the ship or the airplane, simultaneously trying to point out the ship or the airplane to sixty people who could see nothing but a mountain scene. It was loud, demonstrative, and needless to say a lot of fun, but unfortunately quite unproductive.

It did not matter how loud you shouted, how much you pointed to the area on the painting where the ship was, most of the people there could not see what I thought was so obvious. I never saw the airplane. Some who easily identified the airplane just could not see my ship, and most just saw the mountains . . .

The lesson I learned from that class in the sleepy Ozark Mountains has never left me. It is an undeniable fact that people can look at the same thing and see something completely different. Something that is so clear to you, others may see in a completely different light, or, may not be able to see at all. And vice versa, though we may not like to admit it, others may be able to see something that we cannot see at all.

You may totally disagree with all or part of this book.

At one time in my life, that thought may have offended me, but not since the day I saw the mountain picture.

- Some of you will never see some of the things I am going to write about in this book.
- Some of you will be offended that I would even suggest some of the things I will write about.
- Some of you will see/understand because what I am writing about is happening in your life right now.
- Some of you will say amen, because you have experienced some of the things I am addressing.

A Word From The Author

- Some of you, somewhere in your future, will walk down memory lane and remember excerpts from this book as you experience these things for yourselves.

****

Questions on my Mind

Once, when asked why God allowed so much human pain and suffering on Planet Earth, Mother Theresa, the world renowned missionary to Calcutta replied that when she eventually died and went to heaven, the first thing she was going to say to God was, "You've got a lot of explaining to do."

I imagine the question line will be very long in front of God's throne, as everyone will have questions for Him. All the lifetimes of wondering why things happened as they did . . . all the answers readily available, no more wondering. What questions have lingered in your mind over the years that you would love to pose to God?

I think that while I wait for the line in front of God's throne to diminish, (of course this is assuming and hoping that I make it through the pearly gates), I will go look for King David and John the Baptizer, because I have questions for both of them.

I would like to ask John, "After you baptized Jesus, you saw the Spirit descend on Him, and heard the voice from heaven declaring Him to be God's beloved Son. Then you pointed to Jesus and declared to your disciples, "Behold the Lamb of God which takes away the sins of the world." The next day you were with two of your disciples, you saw Jesus, you said to your two disciples, "Look, the Lamb of God."

YOUR PASTOR NEEDS THIS BOOK

Your two disciples left you and went to follow Jesus; my question to you, John, is this, "Why didn't you go with your disciples and follow Jesus? Why did you continue to do your own thing?" This has puzzled me for forty years; I would love to know the answer. It just seems to me that you would have been a perfect candidate to be one of the twelve.

To the man after God's own heart, the beloved King David, I would ask: "David, why didn't you go off to war when your men did? Why did you choose to stay at the palace in Jerusalem that fateful spring day?"

2 Samuel 11:1 [NIV] In the spring, at the time when kings go off to war, David sent Joab out with the king's men and the whole Israelite army. They destroyed the Ammonites and besieged Rabbah. But David remained in Jerusalem.

2 Samuel 11 details a very dark period in David's life. Contrary to what some may think, the problem did not start with Bathsheba, the problem started with David's decision to not lead his men into war. David, why didn't you go to war?

Here are just some of the consequences of that decision:
- Adultery with Bathsheba
- Murder of Uriah
- Death of his son by Bathsheba
- Sword to never depart from his house
- Out of David's household calamity would come
- David's wives to be given to someone close to him.

Just as with David, any man/minister who commits adultery will do so only after making some other very bad decisions.

A Word From The Author

If someone were to walk up to me and ask why I committed adultery, I could not answer the question with a fifteen-word sentence. In fact, after seventeen years of soul searching, I would have to say that a series of things came together in my life that made adultery possible. Several decisions I had made prior to that point, allowed me to make the decision to walk down the road to the lust of the flesh.

This book contains my reflections on a process that caused me to commit a sin that has since affected my entire life.

I have no intention of convincing or converting anyone to my point of view. I wish only to share my story.

Focus on the Family has reported that we in the United States lose a pastor a day because he seeks an immoral path instead of God's, seeking intimacy where it must not be found. F.O.F. statistics state that 70% of pastors do not have close personal friends, and no one in whom to confide. (http://www.parsonage.org/)

Should that be your circumstance, no close personal friend, and you need a sounding board, rj@fourbellspublishing.com.

The Law of Temptation

I find then a law, that, when I would do good, evil is present with me. Romans 7:21 [KJB]

For the desires of the flesh are against the Spirit, and the desires of the Spirit are against the flesh, for these are opposed to each other, to keep you from doing the things you want to do. Galatians 5:17 [ESV]

Right off the bat let me address the question, "Who does the Law of Temptation apply to?" Who among us is going to be tempted? Who is going to feel the sinful ropes of lust surround our hearts and attempt to drag us into the sinful abyss of adultery?

In the twelfth century Bernard of Chartres is credited for saying, "We are like dwarfs on the shoulders of giants." Bernard was making the point that we can see farther and know more than those who have lived before us, not because we are smarter or more enlightened, but because we are standing on the shoulders of great men who came before us.

There are three great men mentioned in the Bible whose shoulders I would like for us to stand upon as we attempt to get a very clear view as to which men living among us are subject to the Law of Temptation.

As Winston Churchill said, "The further backward you look the further forward you can see." If this statement is true, and most great minds agree that it is, then history becomes the greatest witness that can be called upon to testify concerning the future.

The Law Of Temptation

Solomon the Wise Man

Here is the legacy/testimony of the wise man, Solomon.

1 Kings 11:3 [NIV]
He [Solomon] had seven hundred wives of royal birth and three hundred concubines, and his wives led him astray. As Solomon grew old, his wives turned his heart after other gods, and his heart was not fully devoted to the Lord his God, as the heart of David his father had been.

Samson the Strong Man

Who numbered among us has not preached about Samson and Delilah.

Let's let the Strong man testify.

Judges 16:18-21 [NIV]
18 When Delilah saw that he had told her everything, she sent word to the rulers of the Philistines, "Come back once more; he has told me everything." So the rulers of the Philistines returned with the silver in their hands. Having put him to sleep on her lap, she called a man to shave off the seven braids of his hair, and so began to subdue him. And his strength left him.
21 Then the Philistines seized him, gouged out his eyes and took him down to Gaza. Binding him with bronze shackles, they set him to grinding in the prison.

David the Spiritual Man

Only one man in history holds the title, "A Man after God's own Heart", the beloved King David. This is one of David's personal life experiences.

2 Samuel 12:9 [NIV]
9 You struck down Uriah the Hittite with the sword and took his wife [Bathsheba] to be your own. You

killed him with the sword of the Ammonites. Now, therefore, the sword will never depart from your house, because you despised me and took the wife of Uriah the Hittite to be your own.

Standing on the shoulders of these three great men, history raises its voice and preaches this undiluted message of truth.

It does not matter how wise you are, how strong you are, or how spiritual you are, you will be tempted.

Regardless of our denomination or religious conviction one thing is true of every man: we all face the same temptations. If you are a man, you will be tempted with lust for women.

I was flipping channels recently and heard a television minister say this: "You can put a beautiful naked woman in front of me and I would not be tempted to sin." I will not mention his name, but I will say that he said this on a nationally televised program in front of the entire world.

Sometimes good positive preaching borders on stretching the truth a little to make a point, and then sometimes preachers may, in the spirit of the moment, make a bold statement in faith. But to insinuate that you, as a man, are beyond being tempted by a beautiful naked woman is just wrong. Forget the being naked part; just a beautiful woman has the ability to get a man's mind headed in the wrong direction. I plead guilty to looking and wondering, so please, do not parade naked, beautiful women in front of me.

When preaching, you should always remember; Exaggeration misleads the credulous and offends the perceptive. ~Eliza Cook~

The Law Of Temptation

The real danger of preaching that you cannot be tempted by a beautiful, naked woman is that you set the bar so high that it is impossible for us, as men, to reach. And it sets up false expectations. If we never reach the prescribed bar, we will always feel like failures as Christian men. However, the other thing is, that kind of arrogance opens the door to the enemy, daring him to make it happen.

I wish there was a place in our Christian walk where we become immune to temptation. To even insinuate that there is a level of spiritually that puts you beyond temptation borders on false doctrine. Come on TV preacher guy, get real …….. You are not above temptation, nor are you greater than Jesus……And women tempted Jesus.

Women tempted Jesus.
I'm sorry if that statement offends you, but it is scriptural.

Our Savior had a duel nature; He was the Son of the living God and yet he also had a human nature. In fact, <u>scripture says He was tempted in all things just as we are</u>.

Matthew 1:18 [NIV]
This is how the birth of Jesus Christ came about: His mother Mary was pledged to be married to Joseph, but before they came together, she was found to be with child through the Holy Spirit.

So this proves Jesus was also the son of man, because His mother, Mary was flesh and blood.

Mark 1:1 [NIV]
The beginning of the gospel about Jesus Christ, <u>the Son of God.</u>

YOUR PASTOR NEEDS THIS BOOK

Matthew 11:19 [NIV]
The Son of Man came eating and drinking, and they say, "Here is a glutton and a drunkard, a friend of tax collectors and sinners." But wisdom is proved right by her actions.

As the Son of God, he healed the sick, walked on water, fed the five thousand, opened blind eyes, turned water to wine, cast out the evil spirits, cleansed lepers, confounded the wise, rose from the dead, and ascended up into heaven.

As the son of man, he knew hunger and thirst, he became tired, he slept, he experienced anger, skinned his knees when he fell, suffered pain and agony on a cross, and ultimately grew from a tiny baby to a teenage boy and into a full grown man, and somewhere along the way looked and wondered about women. As the son of man, he was exactly like every man who has ever walked the earth since the time of Adam.

Hebrews 4:15 [NIV] For we do not have a high priest who is unable to sympathize with our weaknesses, but we have one who has been tempted in every way, just as we are—yet was without sin.

If Jesus was tempted, in every way, just as we are, I can draw two great truths from that verse:

1. **Jesus was tempted by women.**
2. **If Jesus was tempted by women, I certainly will be.**

This is reality speaking here, not faith and hope— simple reality.

If I were to stand before a crowd of 500 God-fearing men and ask this question, "Who in this crowd has lusted after a woman other than your wife?"

The Law Of Temptation

(By the way, never ask this question with wives present because I guarantee you that no hands will go up.) [Smile] Remember back in the old days at altar service preachers would say, "Bow your head and close your eyes." If you ask the question of lust with no one watching, you will probably get more truthful results. [Smile] Maybe half of the men would then raise their hands in response to the question of lust. <u>The other half are lying</u> . . . There are questions that we avoid asking, and the reason we avoid asking these questions is that we do not like the answers. There are issues that we want to avoid--truth we do not want to face.

And the truth of the matter is this, as men, we look at and are tempted by women.

When I was a pastor, I would have had a very diffi-cult time raising my hand in answer to that question. I would have felt as though I was admitting to a spiritual weakness. I felt that raising my hand would have been a bad witness to any Christian man who saw my hand raised. If any of my parishioners had been present, I would've been very embarrassed to admit such a thing.

But the truth is that we have all looked and lusted.

Quote....

I've looked on many women with lust. I've committed adultery in my heart many times. God knows I will do this and forgives me. President Carter---1976

You need to underline what I am about to say and remember it . . . <u>it is not a sin to be tempted. But it is a sin to yield, surrendering to the temptation</u>. As long as there is still a battle raging, all is well. The danger comes when there is no battle. You cannot allow the impure thoughts to become acceptable. There needs to be a struggle going on. If impure thoughts become acceptable in your mind, you are surrendering valuable real estate, your mind, to your enemy, the devil.

Do you think you're on an island all by yourself, because you've looked at a woman and had thoughts you're not proud of? Do you look around at Christian men you respect and think: They're so much more spiritual than I am. They don't think the kind of thoughts that are racing through my mind.

Wrong! We are all made of the same dirt.

When I had just started walking with Jesus, there was a pastor who took me under his wing. He would let me hang out with him, which was quite an honor. He is still a great pastor. Even to this day I admire him. But back in my early days, I thought he walked on water.

One day we were having lunch at one of our frequent lunch spots; I was twenty and newly married. He was forty-something with two children. A young Christian hanging out with a seasoned veteran. Our waitress that day was drop-dead gorgeous. And try as I might, I could not help but glance at her much more than I should.

But the thing that I found amazing, and almost unbelievable, was the fact that I, on several occasions, saw the seasoned veteran looking out the corner of his eyes at the beautiful waitress. That day has always stayed in the back of my mind. You see, we are all the same.

Trust me, the godliest men you know do look at women. You are not a second-rate Christian, you are not un-savable, and you are not a hypocrite. You are a red-blooded Christian man, made out of flesh, that can be tempted, and you need to wrap your head around that. If you do not, guilt will set in. And you will throw your hands up and surrender.

After living for God for years, shouldn't we reach a place where lust can not affect us? Isn't there a place that we as men reach in God, where we do not even briefly have thoughts that are impure? Isn't there some type of spiritual shield that can be wrapped around us to shield us from lust? Isn't there a Bible verse that we can repeat over and over that eradicates lustful thoughts?

<u>Sorry guys. God neglected to create a shield against lust</u>.

You would think that age would make a difference; surely in a man's old age the lure of women should diminish--<u>wrong</u>.

Look at 1 Kings 1:1-2 [NIV]
Don't you just love the way the Bible shows the frailties of the human nature and not just the spiritual exploits? At this point in his life King David was quite elderly and dying. This is the same David who was called a man after God's own heart.

1 <u>When King David was old and well advanced in years</u>, he could not keep warm even when they put covers over him. So his servants said to him, "Let us look for a young virgin to attend the king and take care of him. She can lie beside him so that our lord the king may keep warm."

David was dying and his servants were trying to think of anything that would revive David. Bear in mind that David's servants knew their master. They had observed his life not just outside his chamber, but also inside. Apparently they were aware of David's exploits with women.

YOUR PASTOR NEEDS THIS BOOK

"So his servants said to him." Here they are addressing David. Their suggestion? "Let us look for a young virgin to sleep with you to keep you warm."

Isn't it amazing how men will not fight the suggestions of sleeping with women if the suggestion seems to indicate that it is for a greater good? Here, David is being asked, by his servants, to sleep with a beautiful, young virgin for warmth. Can't you just hear David say, "I will sleep with her at your insistence, but only because you are concerned about my health."

In Genesis 16:1-2 [NIV] Abraham was being <u>asked by his wife</u>, (now guys--it can't get much better than this), to sleep with another woman in order to conceive a child.

1 Now Sarai, Abram's wife, had borne him no children. But she had an Egyptian maidservant named Hagar; so she said to Abram, "The Lord has kept me from having children. Go, sleep with my maidservant; perhaps I can build a family through her."

Abraham, the Father of the Faithful, offered no resistance, to his wife's bizarre suggestion. Not one word.

In the previous chapter, Abraham had a wonderful spiritual experience. God talked with him, telling Abraham that his seed would be as the stars of the sky. God described in detail the land that He would give his descendants. You can not tell me at this juncture, that Abraham doubted that the seed would come through Sarah. He knew it would.

One chapter later, the Father of the Faithful never mentions a word of this. He sleeps with Hagar. To this day we are still seeing the awful ramifications of

The Law Of Temptation

his behavior. There is nothing new under the sun; we as men have not changed.

At seventy years of age you would think David would say something like, "No, it would not be proper for the King of Israel to sleep with anyone other than <u>one of his wives.</u>" There was no resistance on David's part; <u>even in his old age David enjoyed the thought of a beautiful woman in his bed</u>.

The servants basically said, "If anything will revive David, it is a beautiful woman." They searched throughout Israel for a beautiful girl and found Abishag.

Look at the logic of David's son, Adonijah, in verse five. After seeing that even the beautiful woman, Abishag, could not revive his father, David. Adonijah said, "I will be king." To put this in our vernacular, Adonijah said, "If my father, David, can't be aroused by a beautiful woman, David is just about dead, and I will be king."

David was thirty years old when he became king, and he reigned forty years. (Do the math: 30+40=70 years old.) 2 Samuel 5:4 [NIV]

At seventy years old King David was still attracted to beautiful women. So guys, it looks like the fight is for a lifetime. In other words you will have a battle on your hands all the days of your life.

<u>Stay alert</u>! Watch out for your great enemy, the devil. He prowls around like a roaring lion, looking for someone to devour. 1Peter 5:8 [NLT]

Peter refers to the devil as, "Our Great Enemy."
Peter refers to this great enemy as a lion. The lion is of the cat family; cats are great stalkers. And the lion is the king of the stalking family.

YOUR PASTOR NEEDS THIS BOOK

You may not be able to see your <u>great enemy</u> any where around you at the present, but know this one thing, <u>you are being stalked</u>. Right now as you read this book, <u>you are being stalked</u>. Tomorrow at work, <u>you will be stalked.</u> At the grocery store, <u>you will be stalked</u>. At the gas station, <u>you will be stalked</u>. And yes, even while you sit on a church pew, in the presence of God, <u>you will be stalked</u>.

You will have a fight on your hands until the end, because your adversary, the devil, will never give up until you've breathed your last breath. He knows the nature of man; he has observed us from the Garden of Eden. So let me advise you <u>to stay alert, and watch out</u>.

He has your number, and he will dial your number when he thinks it best serves his purposes. Note: time means nothing to your enemy. Just as a cat crouches in the grass awaiting the best opportunity to pounce on his prey, so the enemy of your soul patiently awaits the perfect time to attack you with lust.

The one infallible truth that makes us Christians is the fact that we believe Jesus Christ is the Son of God. As the Son of God, divinity was robed in flesh, and walked the earth among men, and was tempted through the flesh.

If Satan tempted the Son of God, get real, Satan will come after you with a passion. Luke 4 [NIV] records what we refer to as the temptation of Jesus in the wilderness.

The Temptation of Jesus

1 Jesus, full of the Holy Spirit, returned from the Jordan and was led by the Spirit in the desert,

The Law Of Temptation

2 where for forty days he was tempted by the devil. He ate nothing during those days, and at the end of them he was hungry.

3 The devil said to him, "If you are the Son of God, tell this stone to become bread."

4 Jesus answered, "It is written: Man does not live on bread alone."

5 The devil led him up to a high place and showed him in an instant all the kingdoms of the world.

6 And he said to him, "I will give you all their authority and splendor, for it has been given to me, and I can give it to anyone I want to.

7 So if you worship me, it will all be yours."

8 Jesus answered, "It is written: Worship the Lord your God and serve him only."

9 The devil led him to Jerusalem and had him stand on the highest point of the temple. "If you are the Son of God," he said, "throw yourself down from here."

10 For it is written: "He will command his angels concerning you to guard you carefully;

11 they will lift you up in their hands, so that you will not strike your foot against a stone."

12 Jesus answered, "It says: Do not put the Lord your God to the test."

13 **When the devil had finished all this tempting, he left him until an opportune time.**

You should read and never forget verse 13, note especially the last seven words of the verse. He left Him until an opportune time; the ISV says it this way: "He left him until another time." The KJV says, "He departed him for a season."

Regardless of which Bible version you prefer, the same thought is very clear: Satan was not going to stop tempting Jesus! He was simply going to look for a better opportunity to ensnare Him.

YOUR PASTOR NEEDS THIS BOOK

The enemy watched and waited for twenty years before he found the perfect time in my life to tempt me with adultery. At that point several things came together and I apparently met the criteria necessary to be listed on the devil's hit list as a possible candidate for adultery.

What was my adversary waiting for? I think I have identified some very dangerous, and yes, even fatal situations that can occur in your life that make you prey for the Roaring Lion. In my simple way I am going to try to point these situations out to you.

If patience was the only virtue needed to make it into heaven, Satan would have a front row seat on the streets of gold. He shows endless patience waiting for the "opportune time" to lure you to the forbidden fruit he offers.

There are two things that I would like to point out to you about the temptation of Jesus. I think both will be of benefit in your quest to overcome temptation.

#1 When did the temptation of Jesus start?

First, I would like to emphasize the point in His life when Jesus was most vulnerable, most likely to be targeted by his adversary and attacked with temptation. To understand the "when," will also shed understanding on the "why."

Here is the sequence of events that led up to the temptation of Jesus in Luke 4.

- In Luke 3 John declared that he [John] was not the Christ
- John baptized his cousin, Jesus
- John saw the Holy Spirit descend upon Jesus
- John recognized Jesus to be the Christ

The Law Of Temptation

- Jesus went into the wilderness
- Jesus was tempted
- **Jesus began His ministry on earth**

Jesus was no threat to the powers of darkness as long as he was in Joseph's carpenter shop in Nazareth, repairing broken doors and building furniture. As long as he was doing the work of his stepfather, Joseph, all was well; the king of hell was not concerned. But when Jesus came from Galilee to the Jordan in Matthew 3, to be baptized by John, life for Jesus was about to change drastically.

He who was no threat to the powers of darkness while he labored in the carpenter's shop, was about to announce his retirement from the carpenter's shop. Jesus was about to embark on His Father's business.

Luke 2:49 [KJV]
And he said unto them, "How is it that ye sought me? Whist ye not that I must be about my Father's business?"

It was not just John the Baptizer who saw the Holy Spirit descend upon Jesus; the devil also observed the occasion with great interest. He understood the importance of the ceremony. The Father in heaven was giving His Son, on earth, the approval to begin His mission on earth.

At that point the devil decided to stop the program before it could get started. That was the reason for the intense temptation of Jesus in the wilderness; he wanted to stop the gospel from going forth.

As a pastor/preacher you need to understand that when you declared your calling to preach the gospel, the devil painted a great big red bulls-eye on your back. You suddenly became very important to him.

YOUR PASTOR NEEDS THIS BOOK

You were a threat to his purpose. If the devil can stop you, he will also affect the lives of every person to whom you would preach the gospel over your entire career.

Consider this: over your lifetime, you will come into contact with and influence hundreds or even thousands of souls. You need to understand clearly the kind of threat you pose to the kingdom of darkness.

The devil is a skilled chess player; he knows certain pieces on the chess board of life can pay him larger dividends than others. And you, preacher of the gospel, pay the highest dividends. You may as well buckle your seatbelt and get ready; the devil is out to wreck your life. You are on his priority hit list. The devil knows very well the concept that Jesus was referring to in Matthew 26:31, [NIV] "Strike the shepherd, and the sheep of the flock will be scattered." As a Pastor, if the devil can de-rail you, he will also cause havoc among the people you are leading.

According to the Francis A. Schaeffer Institute of Church Leadership Development you have entered into a very dangerous occupation.
www.intothyword.org

Pastor, you really need to read these statistics and then re-read them. You really need to take this to heart, because it is no joking matter. You also need to lose the, "It can't happen to me mentality." The king lion loves prey that wanders through life oblivious to its situation.

Excerpt from, Statistics on Pastors

After over 18 years of researching pastoral trends and many of us being a pastor, we have found (this data is backed up by other studies) that pastors are in a dangerous occupation! We are perhaps the single most stressful and frustrating working profession, more than medical doctors, lawyers, politicians.

The casualty rate is alarming in the ministry.

Again, statistics from FASICLD,
Nine hundred thirty-five, (935 or 89%) of the pastors we surveyed also considered leaving the ministry at one time. Five hundred ninety, (590 or 57%) said they would leave if they had a better place to go—including secular work.

Of the one thousand fifty [1,050 or 100%] pastors we surveyed, every one of them had a close associate or seminary buddy who had left the ministry because of burnout, conflict in their church, or from a moral failure.

Thirty-five to forty percent of pastors actually do leave the ministry, most after only five years.

Let the numbers sink in, 89% have considered leaving the ministry at one time or another. 57% said they would leave if they had another job to replace their current job with. 35-40% do leave with in five years of beginning ministry.

It is not by chance that we, as preachers, are falling by the wayside. There is a spiritual war going on, and your adversary has you in his cross hairs. The sad thing about this entire scenario is that while the war in the spirit world is raging for our souls, we are not even aware nor do we believe it is really happening.

The harsh truth is that we have been lulled to sleep spiritually, by the diluted gospel that we find our-selves preaching and believing. It is impossible to believe that there is a big bad devil out to destroy you if you are questioning the very basics of the book you preach from.

YOUR PASTOR NEEDS THIS BOOK

Jesus survived the temptation in the wilderness using only one weapon, the Word of God. Jesus believed and spoke the Word, and we need to follow suit. Jesus understood His enemy was out to destroy Him. Jesus resisted, or if you please, battled His enemy with the Word, again, and we need to follow suit. What better example could we have than Jesus? Three times Jesus said, "It is written." We need a fresh baptism of faith in the written Word of God. It may be the only thing that can save us from the conniving machinations of the devil.

Look at it this way. If you are walking through a field at night and you know beyond a shadow of a doubt that there is an open pit somewhere in that field, you will exercise extreme caution as you navigate the field. You will be very careful because you believe you face real danger. If somehow you can come to believe that there is a devil who wants to stop you from preaching the gospel, I think you will use more caution, be more alert and aware of his traps. Knowledge is power; use it to your benefit.

Jesus was attacked with temptation by his adversary because of the mission He was about to embark on. You will be targeted for the same reason. I am convinced that the casualty rate in the ministry is the direct result of a well-planned and strategically orchestrated satanic attack.

YOU HAVE A RED X ON YOUR BACK, PREACHER

The second fact I want to address concerning the temptation of Jesus is this.

#2 Temptation is for a season.

It appears to me that temptation has a beginning and an ending. Verse two, "Where for forty days he was

The Law Of Temptation

tempted by the devil." Verse thirteen, "When the devil had finished all this tempting, he left him."

Jesus was under attack, tempted, for a period of forty days. Matthew, Mark and Luke all talk about the forty days of temptation. It is my opinion that every temptation has a beginning and an ending. The temptation starts, you fight it, it ends, and you get a break. Paul compares our battles to a wrestling match.

Ephesians 6:12 [KJV]
For we wrestle not against flesh and blood, but against principalities, against powers, against the rulers of the darkness of this world, against spiritual wickedness in high places.

I see temptation as a wrestling match, with an intense struggle, then a breather, then a struggle, a breather, then a struggle. This continues until some-one either surrenders or is overpowered. If neither of these things happens, the match is over, until the next fight. This wrestling match will continue all the way to its culmination as described in Revelation 20:10, [NIV] And the devil, who deceived them, was thrown into the lake of burning sulfur, where the beast and the false prophet had been thrown. They will be tormented day and night for ever and ever.

**John records the end of temptation; it ends when the
tempter is defeated. Until then, we fight.**

After the forty days of temptation, the match was over, and Jesus did not surrender, neither was He overpowered. But neither did the devil surrender or give up; the devil just conceded that he could not win at that time. He left to look for a better opportunity.

YOUR PASTOR NEEDS THIS BOOK

While wrestling the temptation of lust, the following ancient proverb may be one of our greatest consolations: "This too shall pass."

Maybe the writer of Ecclesiastes understood life much more than we give him credit for when he penned these words: There is a time for everything, and a season for every activity under heaven.

It is my prayer that you do not surrender in your season of temptation as I did. Your life will be marked forever if you surrender. To that fact I can stand and testify.

Romans 7:21 [KJV]
I find then a law, that, when I would do good, evil is present with me.

Galatians 5:17 [ESV]
For the desires of the flesh are against the Spirit, and the desires of the Spirit are against the flesh, for these are opposed to each other, to keep you from doing the things you want to do.

Our temptations are a result of the desires of the flesh. As long as we are living, breathing, flesh and blood we are subject to the law of temptation. But thanks be to God, one day the fleshly nature will fall away, and we shall be changed into His likeness.

1 Corinthians 15 [NIV]
50 I declare to you, brothers, that flesh and blood cannot inherit the kingdom of God, nor does the perishable inherit the imperishable.
51 Listen, I tell you a mystery: We will not all sleep, but we will all be changed—
52 in a flash, in the twinkling of an eye, at the last trumpet. For the trumpet will sound, the dead will be raised imperishable, and we will be changed.

The Law Of Temptation

This chapter in a nut-shell:

The devil will never stop tempting you.
Your flesh has a weakness when it comes to
women, be on guard at all times.

In the Beginning

In the beginning, not of creation, but of your calling into the ministry, the thought that you would commit adultery never crossed your mind.

It certainly never crossed mine. Just the thought would have been preposterous. After all, we pastors are men with a calling of God on our lives. We have wings growing on our backs, completely unlike "ordinary men."

Does this describe you? Feeling like Superman you donned your red cape with the big S clearly visible on your chest, armed with your faith in God and a very clear vision of the will of God for your life and ministry. You set out to help those in need and to change the world. In the beginning there was no doubt in your mind that you were going to make the world a better place. Failure was not an option; you had God on your side.

Unless you are a minister you can not relate to what we of the cloth refer to as being "called" to labor in service of God. Preaching the gospel is the only vocation on God's green earth that requires an invitation from God in order to be involved. This invitation is referred to as "the calling" by those in the profession.

I suppose the verse upon which we most often base that notion is Jeremiah 1:5 [NIV];
Before I formed you in the womb I knew you, before you were born I set you apart; I appointed you as a prophet to the nations.

In the Beginning

The thought is very clear in Jeremiah, God chooses/calls people to work in His kingdom.

The Apostle Paul shed some light on the reason he preached the gospel. 1 Timothy 1:12 [NASB], "I thank Christ Jesus our Lord, who has given me strength, that he considered me faithful, appointing me to his service." Here Paul says he was appointed by Christ Jesus, and where Paul uses the term 'appointed', we use the word 'called.'

The point I am trying to make is that regardless of your origin, you must be "called" by God to preach His Word. In fact, if God calls you into His service, you alone hear the call. It is a very personal experience.

If you look around you will often see children following in the footsteps of their parents. Carpenters produce carpenters, and doctors produce doctors. But it doesn't work that way in God's economy. God calls whosoever He wills. Many times you will see the son of a minister entering into ministry. Much could be said about that, but not at this juncture.

As for me, I was an Amos.

Amos 7:14 [NIV] Amos answered Amaziah, "I was neither a prophet nor a prophet's son, but I was a shepherd, and I also took care of sycamore-fig trees. 15 But the Lord took me from tending the flock and said to me, 'Go, prophesy to my people Israel."

No one is my family tree stood before pulpits to preach the Good News. My tree was filled with carpenters and building contractors. It was pretty much an assumed fact; I would follow in my father's footsteps and work with him in the family business, the construction industry.

YOUR PASTOR NEEDS THIS BOOK

At age nineteen that made perfect sense. I knew the business inside and out. Some of my earliest childhood memories are of being on a job site with Dad. It would have been a very good career choice.

But for years, there had been something down deep inside me that I mentioned to no one. I wanted to be a preacher. I don't have a clue where that desire came from, but it was there, and little by little it grew stronger. Some men are able to give you an exact time and place when they felt the call of God. I have often heard ministers tell of hearing a voice, or having a dream beckoning them into the service of the Lord. To be perfectly honest, to this day, I probably would not believe those stories, had it not happened to me.

I heard an audible voice that actually spoke my name. I have never told that to anyone, and will leave it at that.

GP

A preacher stood at the door shaking the hands of the parishioners as they left. He had just finished his Sunday sermon. One old man said to the young preacher: "What makes you think you're called to preach?" The young man explained: "I was out working in the field, and I looked up at the sky. Right there, above me the clouds formed the letters 'GP.' I took that to mean that God was telling me to 'go preach." The old man shook his head and said: "I think that meant 'go plow."

There is another version of the same story that says, while plowing in the field, I saw among the clouds two huge letters, GP. I took it to mean "go preach." Now after a lifetime of preaching, it dawns on me, God was really saying, GP, "good plowing."

31

In the Beginning

I believe that, like me, most pastors would have to describe their personal calling as a desire that starts inside the heart. It starts very small, but continues to grow and grow until it seems that working for God becomes all we think about. My calling was a very strong feeling/desire that became so overpowering that I just could not ignore it.

When I was in the eleventh grade I was on a date with a senior, who was about to graduate, the star of the girls' basketball team. I remember it was our first date, and eventually the conversation turned to plans post high school, and we talked about our career ambitions. It was the first time I'd ever verbally expressed what I had kept hidden deep inside for so long. Suddenly I said, "I'd like to be a preacher." I do not know who was more shocked by what I had just said, me or my date. I think it was on that night at sixteen years of age that I pretty well decided what I would do with my life. I wanted to help people; I wanted to preach the gospel.

I think everyone who is a minister will tell you a similar story. We felt a call from God.

At the beginning of your service in The Lord's Army, it was all about faith and prayer; it was all about studying the Word; it was all about finding someone to encourage, and helping the needy. It was preaching anywhere you had an opportunity. It was pure; it was simply and exciting………

I preached my first, official, real sermon when I was nineteen. By that I mean I stood at a pulpit, read a passage of Scripture and talked to the congregation. A very kind-hearted pastor was brave enough to let me practice on his congregation, knowing full well that they were helping me much more than I would help them.

YOUR PASTOR NEEDS THIS BOOK

Forty years later I can still tell you my text and message title.

I read from John 21:15 [KJV] So when they had dined, Jesus saith to Simon Peter, "Simon, son of Jonas, lovest thou me more than these?" He saith unto him, "Yea, Lord; thou knowest that I love thee." He saith unto him, "Feed my lambs."

I titled my sermon, "Lovest Thou Me?"

As with most young, inexperienced, first-time preachers, "I just plain ole dropped the watermelon." I spoke too fast; lost my train of thought, and was so nervous that I knocked my sermon notes onto the floor.

But in spite of it all, I witnessed a miracle happen that night. I saw my thirty-minute sermon miraculously turn into a four or five-minute discourse. Thank God that was before the days of recording and videotaping sermons, because it would be very painful to re-live today. However, I would love to know how many times in that short span of time, that I repeated the words, "Lovest Thou Me?"

The pastor of the church, who was also my pastor at the time, asked me a question later that night, teasing me. "Were you preaching or proposing?" He added that every time I would say, "Lovest Thou Me?" I would look to the left at the beautiful young pianist sitting on the first row.

It was decided several months later that I was in fact, proposing rather than preaching. And the beautiful young woman said yes.

We have now been together nearly forty years. Or perhaps I should say nineteen wonderful years, then one year that is best described as hell on earth, that

In the Beginning

the Lord turned around for good, to make the following twenty years the best imaginable.

Let me make something very clear right now, we are not still married because of anything I can take credit for. We are together because the incredible Christian woman I married has a heart so full of love and forgiveness, that even after I had given up, she would not. Always remember, when it comes to forgiveness, especially when a husband or a wife is in the scenario, you have to have a great big dose of God in your heart to pull off the feat.

It is easier to forgive an enemy than to forgive a friend. ~William Blake~

I am fully aware of the fact that 1 Peter refers to the wife as the weaker partner.

1 Peter 3:7 [NIV] Husbands, in the same way be considerate as you live with your wives, and treat them with respect as the weaker partner and as heirs with you of the gracious gift of life, so that nothing will hinder your prayers.

You will never hear me refer to the woman who carried me on her shoulders when I was too weak to walk, as the weaker partner. But I digress from the beginning of ministry . . .

We were married in April of 1971. We had talked at great length about my calling into the ministry; she was very excited and supportive about being in the ministry. She brought with her talents that would bless any ministry. She sang, played music and had a personality that was to die for; she's one of those women who never met a stranger. She simply loved others.

YOUR PASTOR NEEDS THIS BOOK

Oh, the dreams that we dreamed in the infancy of our wonderful young love.

I was raised in a very conservative church. My dad was never baptized and was not a regular church-goer. He believed in what the church preached, and supported it financially even though he attended only sporadically. My mother was baptized and became a very devoted church member when I was about ten years old. As a result of Mother's conversion, my three sisters and I had no choice in the matter, three times a week we were in church; that was not nego-tiable.

Like most ninth grade boys, I did not enjoy church nor did I want to attend, so one church night I faked an illness. And wouldn't you know it, as soon as my mother and sisters drove away; God came into the room and healed me. [smile]

Since I suddenly felt so much better I saw no need to languish in bed. Across the road from our house there just happened to be a malt shop where area teens hung out. The malt shop had a pinball machine, and I was good at pinball. That was back in the old days when pinball machines actually paid off. You could play for a nickel. If you could run your score up to a certain amount of points, you would win a burger, fries and Coke.

The tension rose as I was getting ever closer to winning the prize and all the kids began to crowd around and cheer me on. I was in the height of glory, just about to cash in, when suddenly, someone grabbed me by the ear and dragged me out of the malt shop. Again, thank God there was no YouTube back then, as I am sure the picture would have gone viral. Mother never said a word as she dragged me to the car, so we could go to church.

In the Beginning

I've always wondered, "Do mothers have X-ray vision? Are they telepathic? How do they know the things they know?" After that particular ordeal I was never again given the benefit of the doubt; I simply went to church sick or not.

My new bride had been raised by devoted Christian parents. Unlike me, she had been raised in church all her life. We both attended the same type of church, and its doctrine was the only one we knew.

In our church organization there were two ways to become a licensed minister. You could attend a Bible school and after completing the courses you graduated as a minister. The other option is what I call the on-the-job training method. You would work under an experienced pastor as an intern (sometimes called an assistant to the pastor). And in case it's not obvious, an assistant to the pastor is a totally different thing from being an assistant pastor.

When my dad realized I was serious about going into the ministry, it was a very difficult thing for him to accept. I am an only son; he wanted me to follow his footsteps in the building industry. As a young man I could not understand why he felt so passionate about it. But now that I have grown older and have a son of my own, I fully understand the longing to keep your son nearby.

My dad was not a great talker; he was a little on the shy side, and somewhat challenging to engage in conversation. When he had something on his mind he would get right to the point, without a lot of small talk. One day he told me to sit down, because there was something he wanted to discuss with me. Well, I knew something was up because he wasn't one to discuss things. He simply told you what he wanted you to do.

YOUR PASTOR NEEDS THIS BOOK

On that particular day he got right to the issue at hand. He said, "If you are dead set on doing this preaching thing, pick out the Bible school you want to attend and I will foot the bill." That was his way of saying, "I accept your decision to become a preacher."

The problem was, my pastor was an older man and he was from the old school. He was anti-Bible school. He felt that if you had a call of God on your life, God would teach you all you needed to know and He would put words in your mouth while you were preaching. And at age nineteen all I knew was that I wanted to preach. I did not have a clue what I should do. At that time I listened to my pastor. In all honesty, if I had it to do over again, I would go to seminary. It is much easier to gain knowledge from many minds than to draw water from a single well.

Over the next several years I used all my heart, mind and strength to serve two great pastors. I worked during the day to support my new bride, but on evenings, nights, and weekends I became the intern, the assistant to the pastor.

My job description became very clear. I would teasingly ask the senior pastor to ask me, "What is your job as assistant to the pastor?" And I would smile and reply, "My job is to make your job easier." They loved that answer.

Oh, the things required of assistants to the pastor! I cut the church yard in the sweltering heat of summer, and then shoveled the snow from the sidewalks in winter. My construction background made me the perfect choice to maintain the buildings. I was also expected to serve as youth director, and on-call Sunday school teacher. I preached every weekend at nursing homes, and regularly made hospital and jail visits.

In the Beginning

My bride was right by my side all the way, along with her duties as soloist, working with the choir and playing music. We were in charge of fundraising events for the church and served on every committee you can imagine.

In our spare time we studied home Bible courses. Of course there was no pay for our work, and we did not expect any. We were just so excited to be working in God's kingdom; we were in training to one day become ministers.

At some point in your internship you must make a huge decision; what will you do when the pastor feels you're ready for full-time ministry?

Here are the choices:
1. Start a church [very difficult]
2. Find a church in need of a pastor [very difficult]
3. Find a pastor who needs an assistant pastor [very difficult]
4. Become an evangelist [very difficult]

Please note: it's tough to become a full time, paid minister. Especially in the beginning when your resume' has practically nothing on it, and when presented, it screams "novice."

Our heart was set on evangelizing. We wanted to travel from church to church, sing and preach and see souls come to Jesus. Armed with a brand new preacher's license, some brand new business cards, and a seventeen-foot Shasta travel trailer, we were ready to go save the world. All we lacked was a church to preach in.

Our pastor had a brother-in-law in Missouri who pastored a small church; he called and invited us to preach a revival for him. As you can imagine we were on cloud nine, anticipating our first revival.

Back in the old days, revivals were from Sunday to Sunday, and you preached every night and twice on Sunday. So basically you needed ten good sermons to make it through the week. I had already prepared more than the requisite number, so that was no problem. The problem was that the pastor was planning on a two-week revival. That second week was one miserable week for this new evangelist.

The church was located in a converted feed store. There were about thirty people there every night. We had driven 500 miles to get there, and after two weeks of preaching we received our first paycheck! We had arrived in the world of ministry, we were legitimate evangelists, and we had the paycheck to prove it. I wish I had kept that check and framed it, $100.00--$50 a week! We were so excited.

Over the next several years that church became a regular stop, and the pastor and I became good friends. I watched them move from the feed store church to a beautiful church facility on five acres.

Later he told me the reason I received the call to come and preach my first revival at his church. It was the seventeen-foot Shasta trailer we pulled around behind our car. He did not have room to house us in his home, and he could not afford to put us up in a motel. Our little Shasta trailer secured us our first revival meeting.

I have many war stories of our early struggles on the evangelist circuit. After one particular two-week revival at a very poor church, they presented us with their offering to us--a Folgers coffee can filled to the brim with mostly coins, a few dollars sprinkled among the coins. We left the can and contents on the pas-

In the Beginning

tor's porch as we drove off late that night. We simply did not have the heart to accept the offering.

Many times we drove great distances to preach, and then when offering time came we just could not take the money. We never felt it was about receiving, and somehow God always met our needs. Those were "faith building days," and they would serve us well in the years ahead.

At one place the pastor and congregation desperately needed $1000 or they were going to lose their building. They paid me $200 for preaching; I called my Dad and told him I needed $800, Dad never ask why, he just sent the money. Mission accomplished-- $200 plus $800=$1000.

At another revival, the pastor desperately needed his house shingled, because it leaked badly every time it rained. He had the shingles but he could not afford to hire someone to put them on. When the revival was over, I rescheduled my next meeting so I would have a few days off. I showed up at his house with my nail apron and shingled his house. We have been lifelong friends.

We basically lived on credit cards in the early days. We would travel until our cards were just about maxed out, then we would stop somewhere and I would work until the cards were paid down. Then we would go out and do it all over again. I suppose we were long on faith and probably short on common sense. But at the time it made perfectly good sense to us, and we were happy.

One summer we were about 1000 miles from home. We were between revivals and we were broke. I do not mean we were about broke, we were dead broke. We had no folding money and very little change. And to make things worse, the plastic was also nearing the red zone.

We stopped in Augusta, Kansas to use a pay phone; understand that this was BC, before cell phones. I put some coins into the pay phone and made the call, and when I put the phone back on the hook, it was like I had hit the jackpot at a casino; money poured out as if the phone was a slot machine. As God is my witness, this is a true story.

My sweet bride said, "We need to call someone at the phone company and tell them what happened," I said, "If you feel like you need to call the phone company, go head and make the call. But while you are making the call, I'm going to thank the Lord for supplying our needs. I will be over at that malt shop across the road ordering us hamburgers, fries and Cokes, with our winnings." BTW, she did not make the call, because the thought of a hamburger and fries overrode her desire to do what was right.

In the old days of evangelizing, if you were staying in a travel trailer or motor home you did most of your own cooking. To offset the expense, the church would bring you what we use to call "poundings." I have no idea where this term came from, but in essence, the church members would bring boxes of food to the pastor and he would give the food to the evangelist.

On one occasion we were preaching in a very nice church, where we were holding four weeks of meetings, seven nights a week. You have to be an old timer to remember those days.

This particular church was a larger church, and very generous; food bulged from every cupboard. We use to tease each other when we would find ourselves being blessed so much, we would say, "God is about

In the Beginning

to send us to some really struggling church that will empty our cupboards."

This kind church was loading us down with groceries. It was a farming area and it was harvest time. The farmers did what they called canning, [why a person would put food in a jar and call it canning I have no idea] and they brought us freshly canned [jarred] fruit and vegetables.

My sweet little bride was moving some of our newly acquired spoils when she let out a gasp and screamed. Someone had blessed us with twelve quarts of canned tomatoes. Floating in the jars with the beautiful tomatoes were huge two-inch cock-roaches! Apparently someone forgot to wash her jars before canning.

There is no mischief in me but I do enjoy a good laugh. We loaded up the exotic food, tomatoes and roaches, and headed to the pastor's house. The jars were in boxes so all you could see were the tops of the jars. We made a big speech to the pastor and his wife about the blessing of God and the goodness of his church and how we just did not have room in our small travel trailer for the pounding. We insisted that they accept the overflow of our bounty.

That night at church, the pastor pointed his finger at me with a huge smile and said, "You will reap what you sow, I will get you back." Come to find out, the sweet lady who had brought us the tomatoes and roaches was mentally-challenged. We poured out the tomatoes, returned the jars and thanked her for her kindness.

I could fill a book with stories about evangelizing, just as could you about your preaching experiences.

YOUR PASTOR NEEDS THIS BOOK

I must tell you about a fellowship meeting I preached in some remote country church in south central Missouri. It was in the heart of the Ozark Mountains.

It had become a tradition for the host church to provide refreshments after the monthly fellowship meeting. At this particular church, after the service was over, we went down to the basement fellowship hall for drinks and sandwiches.

The church ladies had outdone themselves, the sandwiches were stacked high and what an assortment. I was hungry and was really working on one particular stack of sandwiches. I must have been on my second or third sandwich when a sweet little elderly lady smiled and said, "Looks like you are really enjoying my coon salad sandwiches." I smiled as best I could and said, "Yes Ma'am, I am!" Believe it or not I could not finish the sandwich.

Somewhere in our ministry, though I can't quite nail down the date, I matured enough that I was no longer invited to churches out of sympathy. I had reached a place where I was helping them. That was a wonderful feeling. All the hard work and sacrifice was finally paying off.

We discovered that financially speaking, evangelizing could never support us. Full time on the revival circuit really meant weeks preached not money made. Take into consideration that nobody wants revival services around holidays, vacation times, cold winter months, etc., and thirty-five weeks of preaching a year wasn't enough to sustain us. And then revivals were changing, changing from seven nights to five nights, and then to three nights. It had gotten to the place where we had to travel more and book more churches simply to fill the calendar.

In the Beginning

After about five years of struggling, we decided we would build a home and call it a base camp. I would start up a construction business, and we would go out for a couple months at a time, preach and then come home to work and relax.

Somewhere about this time we graduated from travel trailers to motor homes. My wife was also developing an itch, or should I call it a fever--using the word 'baby' in a lot of our conversations. We felt that traveling in a motor home would be easier for children. They could eat or sleep or play as we rolled down the road to our next meeting. In 1977 we gave birth to the first of our two children. By then we had been married six years. By that time most of our friends had already finished having their babies and here we were at the age of twenty-seven just getting started.

In 1979 I received an invitation to preach five nights in a state-wide crusade. We would be a part of an evangelistic team that would travel to five cities and hold services to minister to all the churches, state wide, of this particular organization. It was quite an honor to be asked to speak at these crusade meetings. Usually it was big name preachers who spoke at these types of crusades, and trust me; I was not a big name.

One of the pastors on the committee organizing the crusade was adamant as to who the speaker was to be. He wanted me. I had preached for this pastor at his church, and held a very successful revival. It started as a weekend engagement and turned into a four-week marathon. At that time the pastor was going through a very difficult time and the Lord was giving me fresh new messages that ministered to his needy heart. He later told me that those services saved his church and his ministry.

YOUR PASTOR NEEDS THIS BOOK

It was at his insistence that I had received the invitation to speak. It wasn't like the crusade was just down the road a ways--it was 2600 miles, one way. We really felt eager to go.

We loaded the motor home, locked up our house, and drove 2600 miles for five nights of preaching. In hindsight, I realized that I should've had my head examined. And my smiling, beautiful bride was right there beside me, supporting me all the way.

For some reason I had it in my mind that while we were traveling across the state preaching these crusades, my pastor friend would be with us working as the M.C., and my little wife would be playing the music and singing.

Well, it didn't turn out that small and simple. Along with my wife and I, they had engaged a very popular singing group to travel with us to provide special music. Putting just a little more pressure on me, these singers traveled and sang for big name preachers. They did not know me. As you can imagine I began to feel a little out of my element.

Along with the singers, we were also accompanied by the district superintendent and the district secretary. It wasn't long before I learned that some distinguished, veteran, foreign missionaries would be in the services. I was way out of my league. I should've been sitting in the audience listening to these guys, not standing in a pulpit preaching to them.

I ask my pastor friend, "What have you gotten me into? I am completely out of my environment. I have never preached with so many influential people in the congregation." He said, "You'll do just fine. Just preach the message you preached the first night at my church." Now that was some good advice. But, I had a new sermon that I really felt I should preach.

In the Beginning

Come on guys, you know the feeling; you've got all the wonderful masterpieces that you have preached, critiqued, and polished. You have them down to a science. They're good and you know they're good, and you can preach them in your sleep. They are tried weapons; you can comfortably go to war with them.

And the first night under all that pressure, I needed something tried and true.

The place was wall-to-wall people. The traveling singing group was professional, top-notch, and they nailed it. The district superintendent was the M.C., mature, distinguished, and experienced. He knew how to lead a service; I gave him an A+ for his efforts.

I took two sermons to the pulpit that night, my very best tried and true sermon, and a brand new sermon I had never preached. Just good ole common preaching sense tells me that I should make it as easy as I can on myself in this brand new and challenging situation. But common preaching sense could not overpower the feeling that my new sermon was for that particular night, so I preached the new sermon.

You don't have to tell preachers whether they have done well or not, they know it before you do. And that night, I knocked it out of the ballpark. It was a wonderful feeling; I had not fallen flat on my face in the presence of my peers. [We are so vain in the delivery of sermons.] What really gave me satisfaction was the fact that I had not let down the pastor who had invited me.

The second night was much easier. I was now on familiar ground. It is amazing how just one night of preaching can change your standing. I had preached to foreign missionaries and prestigious district officials; they respected me as an evangelist. I had arrived . . .

After five nights of crusades, I had twenty-eight invitations to preach revivals. This evangelist had died and gone to heaven. There would be no more struggling for us.

I was twenty-seven years old, and had struggled for five years as an evangelist, but for the first time in my preaching career I can honestly say I felt like a success. All the doubts and fears that I had been wrestling with for so long, suddenly vanished in the sunlight of success.

The next two years were our best and most productive on the evangelist circuit. They were good years; we had reached a place of maturity in ministry, and with maturity, comes fruit. We were really making a difference now; we were being a blessing at every church where we preached.

In 1980, with plenty of invitations to preach, I should have been spiritually content. But I wasn't. I was beginning to lose my enthusiasm for evangelistic work. Maybe it was because our son was getting older. Maybe it was the longing for a more normal lifestyle. Maybe it was just the natural desire to put down roots. Maybe it was a desire for some type of financially security. But in any case, we felt it was God, tugging at our heart strings to go in a different direction.

The natural next step would have been to find a church in need of a pastor and begin pastoring. Over the past years we had preached from Florida to Washington State, and we had contacts/pastor friends who could help us find a good church. We strongly considered that option. But down deep inside our hearts, that was not what we wanted.

In the Beginning

Yes, it would have been easy to find a nice congregation with a nice church building and perhaps a parsonage move in and start ministering. We were no longer novices; our resume' was one that spoke loudly of experience. I could now acquire recommendations from men of authority and respect among our denomination.

But as usual, I was long on faith and short on common sense. Why not let our first pastorate be a home missions church! Let's go start a new church! My bride of nine years has a tremendous faith in God, and she believed I walked on water. Together we decided this was the will of God for us. The decision was made; we were going to start a church!

Much of our ministry was spent in "small church U.S.A." Some of our dearest friends pastored small congregations. We had seen first hand the sacrifices that pastors of small churches make. On the toughness scale, there is probably only one thing tougher that pastoring a small church and that is starting a new church.

For the next year we planned and plotted. We continued to travel and preach revivals, but our conversations were different now. Daily we were discussing the new church we were going to start. We now knew what we were going to do, but then the big question was where we are going to plant our feet and build this church of our dreams?

Faith is an awesome commodity; it allows the possessor to see things other cannot see. But it also presented problems; when we began sharing our vision with our family and friends, they could not see what we were seeing. As a result we received little support for the idea. In our nine years of marriage we had lived our life by one principle, being led by the Spirit. And we were not about to change that now.

YOUR PASTOR NEEDS THIS BOOK

In 1978 we had preached a revival for a presbyter. Our church organization is broken up at several levels. There is a superintendent over each state, and the states are divided into sections, that are presided over by presbyters.

One day the presbyter I was preaching for asked me to take a ride with him. He drove seventy miles, and then stopped for lunch. The presbyter had been called by another pastor who needed his counsel; they were going to meet at this café. While sitting in the café booth, waiting for the other pastor to arrive, the presbyter looked over at me with a grin on his face and said, "The reason I ask you to ride along with me today is because I wanted you to see this city. I think you need to come here and start a church."

I was speechless. Was this guy out of his mind? I was an evangelist and I had no intention of settling down and starting a church at that time or any other time as far as I could see. That detour was not on my radar.

Three years later, we had our motor home parked in that city, we did not know a soul there, and no one knew us. For three days we drove the streets asking God if it was His will.

On the fourth day, we looked at each other and said,

"This is our new home."

In the Beginning

This chapter in a nut-shell:

We all have war stories to tell about the early days of our ministry.

Remember the Sabbath

There are 613 commandments that the Jewish people have celebrated and observed throughout the ages, as the law of God. These 613 laws are found in the first five books of what we as Christians call the Old Testament.

The Jewish religion is very different from Christianity; one of the greatest differences is that the Jews do not embrace the New Testament. Neither do they confess Jesus Christ as Lord and Savior.

Of the 613 laws found in the Old Testament, only ten were <u>written by the finger of God</u> on tablets of stone, and <u>personally spoken by God</u>.

Ever wonder where the old idiom, "written in stone," comes from? Yep, you got it-- Exodus. I think the meaning is very simple and self-explanatory: there are ten laws, written in stone, by God, because they were to be permanent, not subject to change.

McGraw-Hill Dictionary of American Idioms and Phrasal Verbs: Carved in stone and engraved in stone; written in stone Fig. <u>permanent or not subject to change</u>.

I find it interesting in Exodus 19 that God had Moses giving instructions to the nation of Israel, telling them to prepare themselves because the next day, God was going to talk to them from Mt. Sinai. They were going to hear the voice of God Himself.

Remember the Sabbath

Moses' instructions to the people:

1. Consecrate themselves
2. Wash their clothes
3. Abstain from sexual relations
4. Keep their distance from the mountain
5. They were not to touch the mountain
6. They were to kill any man or animal that touched the mountain

This was a first--God audibly speaking to His people. They would actually hear His voice, for the very first time. This is not just "another day at the office." Nor was it simply "business as usual." This would be an extraordinary day. The infinite God of heaven and earth was going to speak to His frail, weak, fallen, sinful creation.

What would God say to His people who, by now, had left the bondage of Egypt, and were living in the desert, looking to go to the Promised Land to establish a nation?

His entrance was spectacular! "There was thunder and lighting, with a thick cloud over the mountain, and a very loud trumpet blast. Everyone in the camp trembled. The smoke billowed up, the whole mountain trembled violently and the sound of the trumpet grew louder and louder."

Had we been there we would have done what everyone else did--we would have trembled, in the presence of His greatness.

And on this historic occasion, what did the Lord say? For what reason had God called this meeting? What needed to be said that was so important that God would allow no one other than Himself, to deliver the message?

YOUR PASTOR NEEDS THIS BOOK

Exodus 20 [NIV]
1 And God spoke all these words:
2 "I am the Lord your God, who brought you out of Egypt, out of the land of slavery.
3 You shall have no other gods before me.
4 You shall not make for yourself an idol in the form of anything in heaven above or on the earth beneath or in the waters below.
5 You shall not bow down to them or worship them; for I, the Lord your God, am a jealous God, punishing the children for the sin of the fathers to the third and fourth generation of those who hate me,
6 but showing love to a thousand [generations] of those who love me and keep my commandments.
7 You shall not misuse the name of the Lord your God, for the Lord will not hold anyone guiltless who misuses his name.
8 Remember the Sabbath day by keeping it holy.
9 Six days you shall labor and do all your work,
10 but the seventh day is a Sabbath to the Lord your God. On it you shall not do any work, neither you, nor your son or daughter, nor your manservant or maidservant, nor your animals, nor the alien within your gates.
11 For in six days the Lord made the heavens and the earth, the sea, and all that is in
them, but he rested on the seventh day. Therefore the Lord blessed the Sabbath day and made it holy.
12 Honor your father and your mother, so that you may live long in the land the Lord your God is giving you.
13 You shall not murder.
14 You shall not commit adultery.
15 You shall not steal.
16 You shall not give false testimony against your neighbor.
17 You shall not covet your neighbor's house. You shall not covet your neighbor's wife, or his manservant or maidservant, his ox or donkey, or anything that belongs to your neighbor.

Remember the Sabbath

In God's first conversation addressing His new nation-to-be, He gave the Ten Commandments. Do you think that was an accident? I don't think so. Do you think it was a spur-of-the-moment decision for Him to write laws in stone? Neither do I.

The Ten Commandments
1. Thou shalt have no other gods
2. No graven images or likenesses
3. Not take the LORD's name in vain
4. Remember the Sabbath day
5. Honor thy father and thy mother
6. Thou shalt not kill
7. Thou shalt not commit adultery
8. Thou shalt not steal
9. Thou shalt not bear false witness
10. Thou shalt not covet

To God, the Giver of the commandments, these ten were and still are of such great importance that He instructed them to be stored inside the Ark of the Covenant, under the mercy seat, which represented the very presence of God Himself.

Clearly the Ten Commandments are extremely important to God.

Most of the 613 laws of the Old Testament have now ended; Jesus was the sacrificial lamb whose death on the cross ended the old covenant and initiated the new covenant of faith. In other words, the covenant that began at Sinai, the covenant of the law, ended at the cross. The covenant of grace, with which we are so blessed, started with the cross.

I'm not going to spend a lot of time preaching to the choir about living under law as opposed to living under grace. For us, the eating of clean food versus unclean food is not a concern. The law concerning the spread of leprosy is no longer an issue. Mold or mildew in the house--not a huge concern. The clean versus unclean woman is over and done with. For Christians, there is no need to observe the ceremonial laws.

But the moral laws, contained in the Ten Commandments, are still the cornerstone of our Christian society.

God gave mankind the Ten Commandments on Mt. Sinai to serve as principles of moral behavior for the human race. They will always be the foundation of the moral code and the legal system of justice for Western Christian civilization.

The Ten Commandments will forever be the most valuable mirror that we, as humanity, have to view the nature of God. With His finger He wrote them, and with His voice He spoke them; they came directly from His heart into our lives to reveal to us His divine nature as well as our own sinful nature.

We violate these principles at our own peril. Oh, the truth that I know to be entwined in that statement! I have experienced the forgiveness of God, but, I also live with my violation of the seventh commandment every day of my life. The sad truth is that we never forgive ourselves.

Psalm 51:3 [NIV] For I know my transgressions, and my sin is always before me.

Most of His commands are so simple that they need no explanation. I like that about God; He leaves no room for personal interpretation.

Across the road from my home is a walking trail that I try to walk several times a day. It is about two miles long. I have a walking buddy who is a minister; in fact, we met on the walking trail. He knows nothing

Remember the Sabbath

about my background. Trust me, being an adulterous, former preacher, is not something that you want to talk about to people you meet. Every week, we seemed to run into each other, so we began walking together and became friends.

He likes to talk Bible as we walk. Years ago, he was into word studies, probably still is; he would get on this tangent of going to the Greek or Hebrew to prove to me what a scripture means. Of course, he was doing this for two reasons, one, to convert me, and two, to impress me.

One day when he launched into one of his complex discourses, I said, "Look, if your Bible is so complicated that it takes a Greek and Hebrew scholar to understand it, you need to buy a simpler version of the Bible, maybe one like mine. My bible has a lot of red writing in it, and I can understand it perfectly." He understood exactly what I was saying; Jesus made it simple and easy to understand, so we should too.

The Ten Commandments are simple in the same way; most are one-liners--very basic, leaving no room for interpretation.

The fifth commandment is the only one to which God attached a promised blessing—"that thy days may be long." Number two and number four both seemed to need clarification, so after God gave the commandment then launched into a commentary--kind of like He wanted to be sure we got the point.

Number four, "Remember the Sabbath day and keep it holy," is a very simple, stand-alone commandment, but God jumped in and began to elaborate as though He thought we might misunderstand what He was saying.

YOUR PASTOR NEEDS THIS BOOK

Work six days; do all your work, the seventh day is the Sabbath of the Lord. In it thou shall do no work.

God's interpretation of His fourth commandment:

- You do not work on the seventh day,
- Your son doesn't work on the seventh day,
- Your daughter doesn't work on the seventh day,
- Your manservant doesn't work on the seventh day,
- Your maidservant doesn't work on the seventh day,
- Your cattle don't work on the seventh day,
- Nor does any stranger/visitor in your gates work on the seventh day.

For some reason, God did not want us working seven days. He sums up the commandment by saying, "For in six days the Lord made the heaven and the earth, the sea, and all that is in them, but he rested on the seventh day."

You and I know, God is God, and God doesn't get tired. So the Sabbath, or "rest", was not for His aching muscles and joints. The Sabbath was for us, His creation.

If we were to list the Ten Commandments on a scale of one to ten in importance, the most important would likely be, "Remember the Sabbath." The reason I say that is because the concept, dates back to creation. Before there was a "Thou shall not kill", or "Thou shall not steal", or "Thou shall not commit adultery", there was a rest day. God established the concept long before there was even a nation of Israel in the wilderness.

Remember the Sabbath

And furthermore, God had been observing the <u>rest day</u> all those years, from creation to the wilderness. I know that to be a fact because of the manna story.

He told the wandering pilgrims in the wilderness, on the sixth day, "Pick up enough manna for the seventh day also." His reason for telling them that was very simple: "<u>Sorry, I don't work on the seventh day, and I am the manna maker</u>."

In Exodus 4:23 [ESV] God gives His reason for taking the Israelites out of Egypt: "Let my son go, so he may serve me." They were slaves in Egypt, with no rest days ever. No time to set aside for God, and no Sabbath.

There is an acronym that we often use in our society-- R&R, which means Rest and Relaxation. We use the term when we are over worked or stressed. We say, "I need some R&R." This is the reason God enacted a Sabbath, for R&R. Only God's R&R does not stand for rest and relaxation, it stands for rest and relationship.

The Sabbath is about you getting rest, and you having time to strengthen your relationships with God and family.

For any relationship to thrive, time is, without a doubt, the most important commodity in the building of that relationship.

- If you do not invest time, you will not be close to your children.
- If you do not invest time, you will not be close to your mate.
- In the same way, if you fail to invest time, you will not be close to God.

Some of you are probably wondering, what in the world does the Sabbath have to do with adultery?

YOUR PASTOR NEEDS THIS BOOK

Okay, I will make it as simple as I can. Before you break the seventh commandment, you will probably break the fourth. The Sabbath is about rest and relationship, plain and simple. As with any law, there are consequences for breaking the Sabbath law.

God did not design us to run on a seven-day clock; He made us for a six-day clock. And no one knows creation, better than its creator. If God created us, and I believe He did, and if our design was as such that we had to have rest, and it was, then to violate our design limitations must have consequences. What are the consequences? I believe we see them in our everyday lives.

- Burnout
- Depression
- Suicides
- Broken homes
- Divorce
- Adultery
- Drug addiction
- Alcoholism
- And the list goes on.

There is a reason why statistics indicate that ministry is perhaps the most stressful and frustrating profession of all--even more stressful than the practice of medicine, law, or politics.

In fact, 70 percent of pastors are so stressed and burned out that they regularly consider leaving church work. http://www.intothyword.org

Thirty-five to forty percent of pastors actually do leave the ministry, most after only five years.

They may be the smart ones. [Smile]

Remember the Sabbath

Why is this happening? I point to the 4th commandment. As a group, perhaps ministers violate the 4th more than any other group on earth. I know I did, big time. And if I were a betting man, I would bet on the fact that if you are a minister reading this book, you are also breaking the 4th commandment.

I would also bet it is costing you dearly, particularly in the area of your relationship with God. This is the first relationship to feel the effects of violating the fourth commandment. The next relationship to feel the effects of violating the Sabbath will be those with your family members. They will be put on the back burner as you gallantly go about doing your good works for everyone else, under the banner of pastoral duties.

Consider this:
This could possibly be the first step, of several, that will spiral you down to a level of depravity that you could never imagine was possible.

Man, just stop and look at the schedule you're keeping, right now. How about a little honesty right here . . . ?

I was at a conference years ago and the speaker talked about the qualities needed to be a successful pastor. The speaker said, and I believe it to be the truth, that any successful pastor would probably be the CEO of a company if he had chosen a secular line of work, or he might be running his own small business. I will just point to Peter and Paul, who would certainly fill the bill. That is exactly the kind of men Jesus called.

To succeed in ministry you must be ambitious, a self-starter, motivated, hard-working [sometimes hard-headed] and love what you do. You must have the

YOUR PASTOR NEEDS THIS BOOK

"failure is not an option" mentality, realizing that sacrifice just goes with the territory.

If we search we can find scripture about self-sacrifice, to support our self-destructive lifestyles; of course they may be taken out of context. It is all about balance, I know that now. Back then—well, that's an entirely different story. But the qualities needed to pastor, can also be a two-edged sword without the use of temperance and some good old common sense.

People often joke about how easy it must be to be a pastor; I mean, what can be so tough about working four hours on Sunday? Yeah, right.

I was in terrible shape spiritually, physically and emotionally, on my thirty-ninth birthday, six months before I ultimately committed adultery.

The church I had founded and was pastoring was growing, thriving, moving forward and impacting our community, just as a powerful, New Testament church should. But I was not the reason for the ongoing revival. The church body was made up of good, well-trained, loving people, and it was that body of believers who were getting the job done. I shouldn't have even been in a pulpit at that time in my life, much less preaching, because, to be perfectly honest, I was spiritually dead.

I am not looking for sympathy, or trying to justify my sin; nor am I trying to paint myself as a victim. I am just trying to tell my story as I now see it, and to warn others by pointing out the steps that led to my sin.

Paul does some boasting in Philippians 3: 4-6 [NIV]

Remember the Sabbath

"If anyone else thinks he has reasons to put confidence in the flesh, I have more: circumcised on the eighth day, of the people of Israel, of the tribe of Benjamin, a Hebrew of Hebrews; in regard to the law, a Pharisee; as for zeal, persecuting the church; as for legalistic righteousness, faultless."

What a resume, with sterling credentials.

Let me boast a bit about my life as a church planter. I can without reservation tell you this, you could have searched the world over and never found anyone more sincere, hard working, or dedicated to the work of the Kingdom then I was, at the outset of my church planting endeavor. I was very sincere.

Now listen to what I am saying, sincerity will not exempt you from the consequences of violating the laws of God. You can weigh in at the very top on the "sincerity scale," and still be wrong. When it came to sincerity, dedication to a cause, and hard working, I bowed my head to no-one. I poured my heart soul and strength into building a congregation.

But, I must say, my first big mistake was violating the Sabbath.

I was working crazy hours, overloading the wagon with no concern for the horse. I was the horse, and I was invincible. Seventy to eighty-hour work weeks were not uncommon. That's right--twelve hours a day, and remember, we also work on Sundays.

Many of you are doing the exact same thing as you read this book. Right now I point my finger in your face and tell you that it will be the beginning of your demise. You cannot transgress the laws of God and survive. You are made for a six-day work week, not seven.

YOUR PASTOR NEEDS THIS BOOK

On my thirty-ninth birthday in September, I was in my fifth building program in ten years. We were building a fellowship hall, a kitchen, Sunday school rooms and a lobby onto the sanctuary we had built the previous year.

Of course, with my construction background, I was not about to waste money and let a construction company come in and do the job. We secured the building permits and the men of the church were doing all the work possible while I worked as foreman on the jobsite nine hours a day. It was the epitome of multitasking, which is so coveted in employees these days. I kept a suit in my office while I worked in coveralls as building foreman. When I had to revert to pastor mode for whatever reason-- hospital calls, family crises, counseling sessions, I would hurry into my office, take off the coveralls, don my tie and coat, and race off to the crisis.

Clark Kent had his phone booth, I had my office. We both had the same mindset; we both believed we were Superman!

Along with the building program I preached three times a week in the sanctuary: Sunday morning, Sunday night and Wednesday night. Not long ago Lifeway Research conducted a study of how pastors spent their time. An interesting part of the study was the amount of time they spent on sermon preparation. http://www.lifeway.com

Among ministry activities, pastors spend the most time on sermon preparation. Half of them spend five to 14 hours in sermon preparation. Nine percent say they spend 25 hours or more in sermon preparation each week, and 7 percent report they spend less than five hours preparing to preach.
[From Lifeway Research]

Remember the Sabbath

Of course what needs to be taken into consideration is the number of sermons being prepared. The average prep time is estimated at five to seven hours per sermon. In fact, fifteen hours of prep time is probably a very conservative number. Then add a minimum of three hours at church per service. I was putting in a total of twenty-four hours a week in sermon preparation and church attendance.

Every other month, I spent Monday nights teaching a four-week class for new converts. This class did two things: it allowed me time to instill some basic Bible doctrine into new converts, but more importantly, it allowed me personal time with each of them. It was a very small group setting. I have always felt that it was one of the keys to our phenomenal church growth. I wanted everyone to know that I, as pastor, was very real, and accessible.

I know that this concept is key to church growth, but to this day I do not know where the line should be drawn. Just as a person has time for just so many friends, a pastor has just so much time to give to people/parishioners.

Tuesday and Thursday nights I did outreach. I would go into people's homes, who were not church-goers, and try to win their trust in me as a person, and their hearts to God. My goal was to go into their homes for eight weeks to give them a panoramic view of the Bible.

It is amazing how many people want to hear the Word of God; they just don't want to go to church to hear it. My concept was, "If the mountain will not come to Muhammad, then Muhammad must go to the mountain." I took the Bible to them. If you gave me four weeks in the home of a sincere person I would have them sitting on a church pew by week five. I gloated over my success rate. At times I was in ten homes per week. All it takes is time! I loved that part of my job.

Wednesday nights were set aside for our regular church night, for prayer and Bible study. Friday night was for youth functions. Saturday nights were set aside for choir and music practice. And would church be complete without a baseball, basketball, or volley-ball league? I don't think so. And I participated in all of them.

Let's see now:
- Building program,
- Monday night Bible study,
- Tuesday night outreach,
- Wednesday night Bible study,
- Thursday night outreach,
- Friday night youth functions,
- Saturday night choir,
- Then of course Sunday, [the famed day of rest] including Sunday school in the morning and a Sunday night service.

I must insert here the title of a glorious old song,
"Every Day Will Be Sunday Bye and Bye."

"Oh, bye and bye, bye and bye
Oh, when I reach that home beyond the sky
Far from the land of worry and pain, sickness will never come again
And every day will be Sunday bye and bye."

And all the preachers jumped up and shouted,
"THEN I DON'T WANT TO GO."

Let's see--did I miss anything? Oh yeah-- did I mention I had sold my house and was building a new one? But no problem, it was only two blocks from the church building project, so I could ride my bike back and forth all day long! It was good exercise.

65

Remember the Sabbath

When I turned thirty-nine in September I had already been keeping that schedule for God knows how long. Sometime in October/November of that year, I began to fall apart. I had heard the terms, "midlife crisis", "burnout" and "depression", but at that juncture of my life, I did not see any of these things as my problem. In all honesty, it's much easier to see other people's problems than your own.

Compounding the problem is the fact that we as pastors have to maintain an image—we have to appear as if we're immune to the ordinary trials and problems of life. We must emit the aura of invincibility, which we use to measure both our faith and our manhood.

It is very difficult to describe how I was feeling at that point in my life. If I had to sum up my feeling in one short statement, I would say that I felt very much alone, lost, and tired. I was very tired.

Why alone? I now understand why I felt so lonely. I had no relationship with God at all. Praying, meditating, devotions, quiet time alone with God had all fallen by the wayside. In my quest to save the city, I had forsaken the very basics of walking with God. Pray, Study, Meditate. I had sacrificed these basics <u>on the altar of too busy</u>. And I was about to pay the price.

As a minister of the gospel, if you are too busy to spend time with your Boss, you are too busy, and in time, the Boss will have to fire you. He has no choice. You are no longer an asset to the family business. In fact, by then you will have become a liability.

"My mother's sons were angry with me; they made me keeper of the vineyards, but my own vineyard I have not kept!" Song of Solomon 1:6 [ESV]

YOUR PASTOR NEEDS THIS BOOK

The truth is that if you do not nurture your personal vineyard, it is impossible for you to take care of His vineyard.

God had blessed me with such a wonderful opportunity to preach His good news to others. I was constantly telling them how to have this wonderful, intimate relationship with God, a relationship that I did not have. The harsh truth is that if you do not have God in your life, you will become incredibly lonely, desperate and depressed.

My best friend and confidant of twenty years seemed like a stranger to me. We spent no personal, quality time together. She was busy, for the most part, being a single parent, raising our two children with almost no help from me, to say nothing of managing all her church responsibilities.

I was working the day shift on building programs, and then on the three-to-eleven shift, doing church work. I was gone much more than I was home. We were going through the motions of being married, but the spark had long since died. For far too long I had sacrificed this relationship also, <u>on the altar of too busy</u>.

I had reached the place where I rarely slept; I simply could not disengage my mind. It wasn't long before I began to have panic attacks. The love that had once filled my heart was gone; fear had taken its place. And remember, fear has torment. In my mind I began to question everything, even the existence of God.

I stopped teaching Monday night classes; I stopped Tuesday and Thursday night outreach. I even began to make excuses to avoid church functions. I was withdrawing from people. Every time the phone would ring I would literally cringe and my stomach

Remember the Sabbath

would clench as I felt my anxiety rising. I started avoiding phone calls, because there was no one I wanted to talk to.

I was experiencing a complete personality change. The outgoing, charismatic, upbeat, full-of-faith person that I once was had been replaced with a lonely, quiet, recluse I did not know.

As strange as it sounds, I was in the people business, and yet I found myself, not liking people.

At church services I began to stay in my office until it was time for me to preach or teach. I had a back door entrance to my office with a parking space right beside the door. I could enter the church building and never have to say hello to anyone. It had become my practice to avoid others at all cost.

But how do you preach, you might ask, if you haven't been studying or praying for direction?

No problem. I had a collection of twenty-year old sermon outlines in my office filing cabinet. I remember one Sunday night sitting in my office until the last minute before I had to take the pulpit. I walked to the filing cabinet, opened the bottom drawer, closed my eyes and picked out an old sermon outline and walked to the pulpit. The sad truth is that I was dead spiritually, just going through the motions of ministry.

After church that night I asked one of the senior board members if he would meet with me in my office. This board member was a prince of a man; he had been a member of the church for nine years. He was well-respected and loved by the congregation. I considered him to be my friend, and I still do to this day.

YOUR PASTOR NEEDS THIS BOOK

I desperately needed someone to talk to. I had gone as far as I possibly could.

He ran through all the preliminary courtesies that I always admired about him. "Great service tonight pastor, wonderful sermon." "Didn't the choir do a great job?" "Did you get to meet the new families?" At that point I stopped him. I told him how much I appreciated him as a church leader and as a friend, and then I told him that I needed his help. I still remember the concerned look that came across his face. His response was without hesitation, "Sure, Pastor, anything you need."

He did not know what was coming, but he was ready to help me with whatever the problem was. Friends of that caliber are rare treasures, few and far between, and well worth keeping.

I did not beat around the bush. I told him I was giving him my resignation as pastor, and I needed him to pass the word to the other board members. I would not be preaching anymore, effective immediately.

By the look on his face I knew he couldn't have been more shocked. For what seemed like minutes, he just stood there and looked at me with a shocked, puzzled look. Then I saw the tears glistening in his eyes. But when he asked the inevitable question—"why" I failed to open my heart and really unburden my soul to him. In the process I made a big mistake, violating yet another biblical principle.

Carry each other's burdens, and in this way you will fulfill the law of Christ. Galatians 6:2 [NIV]

Pride is a very dangerous thing; it works in the lives of most men to our great disadvantage. I was too proud to admit the truth to my good friend.

Remember the Sabbath

The only explanation I offered was, "I just don't want to pastor anymore." I remember him saying, "But that makes no sense. You founded this church. You are the only pastor we've ever had. The church is growing, and God is blessing, so why would you want to resign now?"

From my meeting with the board member, I went home to share the news with my wife. As you can imagine, that went over like a lead balloon. My wife is one of the sweetest, kindest women you could ever meet, a true Christian.

Again, I failed to open up and reveal my true emotional and spiritual state. I just told her I was tired of pastoring. She asked, "Well, what will we do if we resign, go start another church? Evangelize again? Shouldn't you find another pastorate before we leave this one? What about the kids?" She was asking a lot of questions I couldn't answer.

I remember telling her that I would like to just go somewhere and get a job; I did not want to preach. I wanted a normal life.

At that point, it was obvious for the first time, we were living in two different worlds. She was walking with God while I was stumbling around in the darkness, lost and very much alone. As we fell into bed that night, hoping for sleep to end the chaotic thoughts in our minds, she said, "Preachers don't just walk away from a church like ours."

I knew that to be the truth; preachers would line up to cast their hat into the ring for the opportunity to pastor our church. You don't walk away from good, growing churches; as a pastor you search for them.

That night I slept for the first time in months. My decision was made, and as far as I was concerned,

YOUR PASTOR NEEDS THIS BOOK

preaching was a thing of the past; I felt good--relieved.

A sidebar worth considering.
Pastors, I know it's difficult to observe a Sabbath when you are on call 24/7. I also know that you're in the gospel business because you want to help people and that means being accessible. But why not have two days a week when someone screens all your calls, so that you take only emergency calls.

And for your personal quiet time with the Boss, how about shutting all phones off? Begin with a new mindset: it's rude for anyone to interrupt your absolutely essential rest time alone with God. Why not hang a sign on your door that says: Do not disturb, I am talking to God. That should stop knocks on the door . . . in a nice way.

If you were in your office with the President of the United States, you would not insult him by answering phones or opening the door every time someone knocked. When you are in conversation with the Kings of kings, you must honor His Deity in the same way. Your time with God is supposed to be a time to transfer the weights and burdens you are carrying onto the shoulders of the everlasting God, and it's not negotiable if you want to succeed.

Matthew 11: 28 [NIV]
Then Jesus said, "Come to me, all of you who are weary and carry heavy burdens, and I will give you rest."

While we are on sidebar, I must address the subject of vacations. For ten years we spent every vacation doing something church-related.

Remember the Sabbath

The reality is:

- Taking your children to a church youth camp is not a vacation.
- Being a counselor at a youth retreat that your children or church children are attending does not qualify as vacation time.
- Camp meetings are not vacations
- Ministers' retreats are not vacations
- Denominational general conferences are not vacations
- Young marriage retreats are not vacations
- Minister retreats are not vacations

If an activity/trip has anything to do with church or church people, you are deceiving yourself if you believe you're resting or vacationing. For ten years we did exactly that. Bad idea.

Repeat after me...."Va-ca-tion, good."
Now let's say it again, "Va-ca-tion."
Now, take it one step further.
Repeat after me: "I need to take va-ca-tions."
"My family needs va-ca-tions."

The word va-ca-tion is defined as:
A period of suspension of work, study or other activity, usually used for rest, recreation, or travel; recess or holiday: ex. Schoolchildren are on vacation now.

Begin to think of your ministry as a battery. While you are working, your battery is being drained. If you put out and put out, give and give, your battery will eventually be drained and have nothing left to give. Rest is your God-given battery charger. I cannot make it any simpler than that.

Why not learn from the Master?

Mark chapter 6 details the first time Jesus sent out the twelve disciples (preachers) that He was person-

YOUR PASTOR NEEDS THIS BOOK

ally training. Up to that time, the disciples were simply observers, sitting at the feet of their new-found Messiah, watching and learning. Perhaps not even aware that they were men in training.

In verse 7, Jesus gave them authority over evil spirits and sent them out two-by-two. Basically Jesus was telling them, "Okay, guys, show and tell time is over. You've been watching me do this long enough. It's time for you to put into action what you've learned. Go preach and help people." Oh, what an exciting day.

Mark 6:12-13 [NIV] They went out and preached that people should repent. They drove out many demons and anointed many sick people with oil and healed them. The disciples came back to Jesus elated at what they had accomplished. They had duplicated what they had seen the Master do. They preached, cast out evil spirits, and healed many sick people. Talk about an inspiring day's work . . . .

They were apparently typical preachers because the Bible records that when they returned to where Jesus was, they gathered around Him and told Him all they had done and taught. There is nothing new under the sun. Want to know what preachers talk about when they get together? You guessed it--they discuss what they have done and what they have preached.

Even back at that time, during a typical day in the life of a preacher, he had no chance to eat, because he was running off of adrenalin and far too busy to eat. This is the part I do not want you to miss. Look at what Jesus did after His preachers had been gone on assignment for only a single day.

Jesus said, "Come with me by yourselves to a quiet place and get some rest." Mark 6:31 [NIV]

Remember the Sabbath

Apparently Jesus understood the stress and strain that accompanies dealing with people. To His devoted twelve, who would inherit the responsibility of preaching the gospel after His crucifixion, He was trying to instill balance, common sense, and principles for longevity of service.

The twelve would have been of no use to the kingdom of God if they started fast, but failed to finish the race set before them, and neither will you. There should be in place right now in your life--safeguards to assure that you, as a minister of the Lord, get adequate rest in your fast-paced and demanding life. It will mean the difference between burnout and long-time service in the Lord's army.

Jesus knew the solution to the problem, time alone to rest.

Mark 4:10 [NIV] <u>When he was alone</u>, the twelve and the others around him asked him about the parables.

Mark 9:30-31 [GWT] They left that place and passed through Galilee. <u>Jesus did not want anyone to know where they were</u>, 31 because he was teaching his disciples.

Luke 18:31 [NIV] Jesus <u>took the twelve aside</u> and told them, "We are going up to Jerusalem, and everything that is written by the prophets about the Son of Man will be fulfilled."

Mark 3:7 [NIV] <u>Jesus withdrew</u> with his disciples to the lake, and a large crowd from Galilee followed.

Here is the thing you need to come to grips with: you cannot save the world. There will always be someone who needs Jesus, a family breaking up, a single mother desperate for rent money, a homeless person sleeping on the streets, or an orphan who makes you

YOUR PASTOR NEEDS THIS BOOK

cry. But you must come to grips and accept the fact that you can't fix everything. Consider this: Jesus couldn't, and He doesn't expect you to, either.

After my first good nights' sleep in months, I woke up with new mountains to face, but I felt good.

As strange as it sounds, I found myself excited about the new possibilities before me. Sure, it was going to take a little time to finish and sell the house I was building. We would have to make decisions about where we were going to move, because we could not very well stay and attend the church we had founded and pastored for the past ten years. That would have been unethical, and also unfair to a new pastor.

I knew it would be difficult saying goodbye to our parishioners and the friends we had made over the years. After all, you don't live somewhere and give ten years of your life and not have some very strong ties.

But all in all, I felt as if a tremendous load had been lifted from my shoulders. I could finally see a light at the end of the dark tunnel I had been living in for an entire year. I really felt upbeat about the decision I had make, and life was good. But that feeling was short-lived. My dearly beloved and the church board had a meeting and decided that I really did not need or want to resign; I was just tired. What I really needed was a good vacation, and afterward I would view things differently, through rested eyes.

I would never deny that their intentions were from hearts filled with love, but the truth of the matter was that I was spiritually dead; somewhere along the way I had backslidden, and walked away from God. And that kind of problem just can't be fixed with a two-week paid vacation, no matter where you go.

Remember the Sabbath

At the end of the two-week break, the outcome was not what I had hoped for. Instead of feeling rested, excited, and ready to get back on the firing line, I wanted out. I remember asking, "Do we have to go home?" Feeling desperate I told my dear wife, "I can't do this. I do not want to pastor." With all the love, faith and hope that a woman could have, she put her hand on mine and said, "It will be alright." But in reality, it was not going to be alright. I would sink deeper into a depression that would lead me to thoughts so dark, that only God could save me.

Hindsight is interesting, but offered little help in the long run. As I look back at that point in time I now know that I was completely burned out. I do not know what would have happened if I had actually stopped preaching and resigned at that time.

That is a question that will never be answered, because I didn't stop preaching. Instead I gave in to the pressure of others. Maybe, over time, I would've recovered and been ready to preach again. But if you want my honest opinion, I do not think so. I think that, regardless of the road I walked down, my preaching days were over. I had run too far, too fast and violated far too many of God's laws.

Within a space of three weeks I had done one of the smartest things I had ever done, and one of the dumbest. The smartest was that I had resigned as pastor. The dumbest was, not following through with that decision. But I just couldn't admit the truth to anyone who could help.

Please do not think that I am in any way blaming the church leadership or my wife for my decision to stay, because that is far from the truth. I made the final decision--I and I alone.

YOUR PASTOR NEEDS THIS BOOK

Sidebar:
At this point I think it's important to offer some steps that will help us as pastors find and maintain a balance in our schedules and our personal lives. First of all, we tend to be very program-oriented, in our efforts to change the world, and there's nothing intrinsically wrong with that. But programs take planning, energy and momentum, as well as help to run them. Over time small projects can grow and loom larger, until a small one becomes a monster, taking ever greater amounts of time, money and effort.

And, though none of us would ever want to nix a successful program, we must consider this question: How many programs does one church need? How long can we maintain the momentum without burning out our overburdened pastors and volunteers? What would happen if we sought God with fasting and prayer regarding the necessity of each program before simply jumping in with both feet?

The thing is, all programs are good, but not all programs are God. If we keep long term mental and physical health in mind, we might perhaps choose to do several small, short-term projects instead of the kind that never end.

Simplify, simplify, simplify. Jesus was a master at it. Preach a while, get away and rest a while. He had no problem keeping a balance. In like manner we need to realize that when we lose ourselves in the process of shepherding our flocks, or if we leave behind God, our families and those we love, we are out of sync with God's will. The hard part is admitting and changing that little equation to get back on track.

A good plan might be for the board and the pastor to evaluate all programs on a regular basis, for efficacy and value. If it no longer works or is overwhelming its

Remember the Sabbath

leaders, it should go, at least for a time. If nothing else, rotate leadership responsibilities, so no one gets overburdened or burned out. Just because we've always done something in the past doesn't mean it's written in stone. In fact, if something is being done simply because of tradition, it probably should end, just because . . .

And speaking of accountability, the board should help the pastor honestly evaluate his own involvement in programs. Some of us tend to be a little obsessive-compulsive, and either can't say no or can't resist a challenge. But the thing to remember is that balance is what will give us long-term staying power. Scripture says the race is not to the swift, but to the faithful, those who actually finish the race. If we burn out, we won't finish—it's as simple as that. We will fall by the wayside because the pace was unmanageable, and that's not at all what God had in mind when He called us into the ministry. In fact, a little dose of sanity might be just what the doctor ordered. (Smile)

***

I remember well the days and weeks that followed the vacation that was supposed to get me back on track. Thanksgiving and Christmas were quickly approaching. I had gone on auto pilot as far as spiritual things were concerned. I did only the duties required--nothing more. I avoided people as best I could. I warmed over sermons from my antique sermon collection and avoided the phone as much as possible.

All my energies were focused on the church building program and building my house. Working with my hands had a way of disengaging my mind, and that is what I longed for--a mind that did not have to think or feel anything.

YOUR PASTOR NEEDS THIS BOOK

I was still chronically exhausted, and I still did not sleep, but I noticed that something new was happening-- resentment was growing inside me. Or maybe it was more than mere resentment. Perhaps the word anger better describes the feeling. Or maybe it was jealousy that was filling my heart.

Just like King Saul, who, in deep depression tried to lead Israel without God's involvement and began to resent David because of God's blessings on his life, I began to resent my wife, my best friend and confidante for nearly twenty years.

Without realizing it I began to hold her responsible for the fact that I was still in the pastorate. But over time the feeling became much stronger than mere resentment. My logic was very simple: if she really loved me, she would not insist that we stay and pastor.

At that point I entered into what I must call the darkest days of my life.

I found myself not wanting to go home; in the same way that I avoided the phone, church people, and pastoral duties, I began to avoid my wife. We were drifting further and further apart. No, that is not quite correct; in reality I was walking further and further away.

The day before Christmas found me on a commercial airline headed to Boston, Massachusetts. I had found a wonderful deal on a small four-passenger plane near Boston. Aviation had been my passion ever since I had first flown at age twenty. I had owned several airplanes over the twenty years that I had been a licensed pilot.

You might ask: what kind of a deranged dad and husband, sleeps in an airport terminal on Christmas Eve away from his family? I did.

Remember the Sabbath

The next morning Nick, the plane owner, was going to check me out in the airplane. That is a pilot term for getting familiar with the airplane. I had never owned or even flown that type of plane before. The check-out usually takes a couple of hours. Our plan was to do a few take-offs and landings to get me familiar with the handling of the plane, then we would spend some time going over the radios and instruments on the control panel.

It was a cold Christmas day in Boston and it was just beginning to snow. I had given Nick the money for the plane and we had just finished the paperwork to complete the sale when the storm hit. He said, "Well it looks like we'll have to wait a few days to check you out in the airplane. This storm should clear out in a day or two." I remember asking him, "Are the tanks full of fuel?" He said, "Yes, fifty gallons." I said, "Great, just show me how to start this rascal, and I'll be on my way."

I will never forget the look on his face when he said, "You're teasing, right?" When he saw that I was serious he said, "You've got to be crazy to take off into that storm." I smiled and said, "No, I'm not crazy. Maybe a little depressed, but not crazy."

For years my habit had been to say a little prayer before lifting off. I still to this day remember the prayer I prayed as I pushed the throttle forward, and the little plane surged down the runway. "Well God, all my life I've heard about heaven, hell, and God. Today I'll find out if it's all true."

I had no intentions of making it home.

This chapter in a nut-shell:

God did not design us to work seven days a week. If you violate your design limitations, you will suffer the consequences, it is the law.

The Actor/Hypocrite

For a man/minister to commit adultery he must cross an invisible line. I cannot put my finger on the exact time I crossed that line, but as I reflect back on my life as a minister, I know I crossed a line somewhere, and at that point I became a hypocrite.

The best definition I can find for the word hypocrite is "actor", someone who pretends to be something or someone he is not.

Actors, to play a part, pretend;

Origin of HYPOCRITE
In Middle English the word "ypocrite", originates from Anglo-French, from Late Latin hypocrita, from Greek hypokrites actor, hypocrite, from hypokrinesthai, one who, like a stage-player, feigns to be what he is not. The term is generally applied to those who assume the appearance of virtue or piety, without possessing the reality. Our Savior accused the Pharisees of hypocrisy.

Long before I tasted the bittersweet fruit of adultery, I had become an actor/hypocrite.

- I acted like I was walking with Jesus, but I wasn't.
- I acted like I was full of the Spirit, but I wasn't.
- I acted like I knew where I was going, but I didn't.
- I acted like I was happy, but I wasn't.

- I acted like I was doing God's work, but I wasn't.
- I acted like everything was normal, but it wasn't.

How does someone who has been a Christian all his adult life and a minister for twenty years become a hypocrite? I am going to make a feeble attempt to explain to you how it can happen, when you are totally unaware that it is happening to you.

<u>Keep in mind that I speak from experience, not from hearsay</u>.

No one likes to be called a hypocrite. To a Christian it's an insult that makes your hair stand on end and your religious blood boil. When someone calls you a hypocrite, they are saying in no uncertain terms that they feel you are not what you say you are.

A good actor will never be called a hypocrite because his performance will be so realistic that he will fool even the most discriminating observer. In the Christian arena it's possible to put on such a wonderful performance that no one would ever dare question your sincerity or your relationship with God.

The Pharisees were masters when it came to acting pious; they knew how to put on a real show. It was not the common man who questioned the sincerity of their words and deeds. The show the Pharisees put on was so realistic that the common man looked at them with envious eyes. They were talented at their performance, acting out their daily prayers and rituals on self-constructed stages of pride and deceit.

It was the Master of the universe who, with the eyes of the Spirit, saw through to their thoughts and their hearts, to detect the Pharisees' true motives and desires. While the crowd oooh-ed and ahhh-ed at

The Actor/Hypocrite

their dedication, the Master saw the Pharisees for what they were. In fact, Jesus wasn't satisfied just to see inside them. He confronted them with the truth, stating categorically that they were hypocrites and frauds.

Like the Pharisees of old, I fooled the crowds with my acting. You may also be a wonderful actor, fooling the crowds. But there was no way I could fool the only one whose opinion matters—Jesus. He knows the heart.

I was fooling the crowds.
No one ever called me a hypocrite, because I
was a very good actor.

I had been preaching and ministering for twenty years, and from that vantage point I can say unequivocally that experience may, at times, become a curse. The more experience a person has, the easier the task becomes so that eventually it requires little thought or effort. I knew how to preach and minister; I had the moves down to a science. Say this, do this, act concerned, ask about the family, show compassion, ask about their problems, visit the hospital, let them know there is hope, preach this, teach that-- you get the picture.

The most melancholy thing about human nature, is, that a man may guide others into the path of salvation, without walking in it himself; that he may be a pilot, and yet a castaway. ~Augustus William~

You can go through the motions of ministry and be very far from God. As I look back now, I realize that at least a year prior to the affair, I was beginning to go through the motions of serving God, i.e. acting as a hypocrite.

YOUR PASTOR NEEDS THIS BOOK

I want to drive this point home: It is impossible to commit the sin of adultery and be spiritually alive!

It is impossible to walk down the road and hold hands with adultery and Jesus at the same time. It simply cannot be done, in the same way you cannot simultaneously go East and West. To embrace either you must let go of the other.

If right now you are committing adultery, don't be deceived; you are not walking with Jesus, and you have absolutely no business attempting to lead others. You should not be standing in a pulpit reading from the Word of God. <u>I certainly had no business there at that place in my life</u>.

I'm sure that right about now there are many who totally disagree with what I just said. Then let me say it more succinctly: <u>it does not matter how long you have been preaching, how large your congregation is, what your last name may be, how many people you have led to Christ, or what you have done in your ministry</u>; there is no place in the pulpit for a man or woman who is committing adultery.

Consider these words from Scripture:
Matthew 7:21-23 [NIV] Not everyone who says to Me on that day, 'Lord, Lord,' will enter the kingdom of heaven, but he who does the will of My Father who is in heaven. Many will say to Me on that day, 'Lord, Lord, did we not prophesy in Your name, and in Your name cast out demons, and in Your name perform many miracles?' And then I will declare unto them, 'I never knew you. Depart from Me, you who practice lawlessness.'

I think one of the great tragedies in the Christian church today is the fact that we have become so tolerant of sin. The Bible is our operator's manual, our road map, and it is God's clear directive on what it means to live godly in this present evil world. I will not argue that some things are more easily understood than others, but on the topic of sexual immorality it is abundantly clear.

Ephesians 5:3 [NIV] But among you there must not be even a hint of sexual immorality, or of any kind of impurity, or of greed, because these are improper for God's holy people.

The harsh truth is that ministry is starkly different from any other profession; it is not just a job. You can be the CEO of a company, be committing adultery, still get the job done, and never get fired. Likewise, you may be self-employed, own your own business, be committing adultery yet still get the work done, and still hold onto your job.

And while that may be true, I'm absolutely convinced that adultery will negatively affect your work. If for no other reason than the amount of time the adultery will consume your thoughts. There are no two ways about it. Adultery is a thought-sucking, attention-grabbing, day-dreaming sin that will totally consume your mind.

This behavior will absolutely take over your life, and again, <u>I'm speaking from experience here</u>. If you have been down this road and are honest, you're saying amen to that statement. Adultery steals your mind, captures your thought life, and enslaves you to the place where you lose the ability to make rational decisions. Every decision revolves around the affair.

In business settings you may be able to do your work and not be fired as you commit adultery.

But that is not so in the preaching business. You cannot perform your duties as a minister and be committing adultery, because your job entails hearing from God through prayer and meditation to determine the words you should say to lead the body of Christ. But that cannot happen because you have ceased prayer and meditation and have no clue what God is saying. In fact, if you're honest you'll admit that you've turned off the wooing of the Holy Spirit. You don't want to hear because you already know what He will say.

If you are simultaneously leading a church, while committing adultery, you have no doubt come to the point where you no longer believe what you're doing is wrong. But if that's the case, be warned, because you have been overtaken by a great deception, convinced that you can do whatever you want and get away with it.

Galatians 6:7-8 [NASB] says this: Do not be deceived, God is not mocked; for whatever a man sows, this he will also reap. For the one who sows to his own flesh shall from the flesh reap corruption, but the one who sows to the Spirit shall from the Spirit reap eternal life.

I was so spiritually dead that I honestly did not think I was committing sin. I can look back now and see these things very clearly. That is a pathetic place for a preacher to be, but it is also a very dangerous place for the flock you are leading. At that point their leader is blind, and he cannot see. I can think of no clearer application of the words of Jesus in Luke 6:39 [NIV]. "Can a blind man lead a blind man? Will they not both fall into a pit?"

That's right; on your downward spiral into sin your sin will blind you so that you will justify your actions and even feel that you deserve the pleasures you enjoy. Note: this is exactly where the devil wants you.

The Actor/Hypocrite

To commit adultery, I had to step off the path where Jesus was leading me and stop following Him. Somewhere along the line I had to stop talking to Him and listening to Him. Somewhere I had to start acting, no longer living my faith, but simply playing a part.

When Jesus used the word hypocrite, it was always in regard to someone in spiritual leadership. In Matthew 15, He spoke about the Pharisees and the teachers of the law. Again in Matthew 23, He was referring to the Pharisees and the teachers of the law. And in Mark 7, His spoke of the Pharisees and the teachers of the law. Are you seeing a trend here?

If Jesus was still alive today, who would He address as teachers of the law? Go to the head of the class if you said, "Pastors and clergymen." <u>The clergy are the modern day, "teachers of the law."</u>

Jesus pointed His finger at them and His indictment against them was very simple and straightforward, "You honor me with your lips, but your heart is far from me." <u>Hypocrisy is a disease of the heart</u>; the heart is not right when a person starts acting, playing a part. At that point sin has somehow gained access to the heart, the seat of our affection and desires.

Does this sound familiar? You honor me with your lips, while you still preach and teach, but that is merely lip service, because your heart [desire, affection] is far from Me. Your mind is elsewhere.

When I refer to the heart, I am not talking about the muscle that pumps blood through the body. I am referring to the seat of our affections, our desires.

The Bible has much to say about the heart. Biblos.com brings up 1223 scripture verses that use the word "heart."

YOUR PASTOR NEEDS THIS BOOK

They include phrases like:
- Pure heart
- Servant's heart
- Broken heart
- Undivided heart
- Wise heart
- Foolish heart
- Joyful heart
- Clean heart
- Faithful heart

And the list goes on and on.

There Are Two Types of Adultery

1. The first is committed with the Heart
2. The second is committed with the Body

As a preacher you might survive adultery of the heart, if you deal with it quickly enough. But you will not survive the physical act of adultery. In reality, if you are committing adultery in the heart, it is just a matter of time before you will have an opportunity to fulfill your heart's desire.

<u>Your days are numbered; you will find a way to bring to reality the fruit of your evil thought life.</u>

In Matthew 5:27-28 [NIV] Jesus points to the culprit of adultery, and it is the heart.

27 You have heard that it was said, 'Do not commit adultery.' 28 But I tell you that anyone who looks at a woman lustfully has already committed adultery with her in his heart.

Again in Mark, Jesus points to the heart as the place where it all starts.

The Actor/Hypocrite

Mark 7:21 [NIV] For from within, out of men's hearts, come evil thoughts, sexual immorality, theft, murder, adultery.

Before you condescend to the place where you actually lie with another woman, you will entertain the thought in your heart. Your heart becomes the battleground. And if you surrender this battleground, you will, in the end, lose the war. Jesus was aware that the heart with its thoughts was the battleground. He also knew that surrendering the battleground, and entertaining ungodly thoughts, causes men to become opponents of the cause of Christ.

Matthew 9:4 [NIV] Knowing their thoughts, Jesus said, "Why do you entertain evil thoughts in your hearts?"

The indictment against the teachers of the law was the fact that they "entertained" evil thoughts. Jesus did not condemn them for thinking evil thoughts; Jesus condemned them for entertaining evil thoughts—big difference. Jesus knew that in order to entertain evil thoughts there had to first be a spiritual decline, a moving away from God in order to make room for what had previously been forbidden. Then that person had to begin to put on an act.

The acting--the hypocrisy, is what enraged the Savior.

It is one thing to briefly think a thought, while it is another thing to entertain that and similar thoughts. When you reach a place where you are enjoying, entertaining, and cherishing, immoral thoughts, you are on dangerous ground. In fact, Scripture says that if we are truly God's, we must take those thoughts captive and refuse to entertain them for even a split second.

YOUR PASTOR NEEDS THIS BOOK

2 Corinthians 10:5 [NASB] tells us: "We are destroying speculations and every lofty thing raised up against the knowledge of God, and we are taking every thought captive to the obedience of Christ."

The old saying is, "You can't keep the birds from flying over your head, but you can keep them from building a nest in your hair." The million-dollar question is this, is there any way to keep the bird from building the nest? Is it possible to keep the lustful thoughts from taking up residence and living in your mind?

Yes, there is, however I can find only one antidote for the immoral thoughts that seek to invade the heart.

Note: If you continue to entertain the thoughts of adultery (or any other evil thought) in your heart, you will reach a place where you will begin to use this logic to take the next step toward the physical act. <u>Here is the logic:</u>
Well, if I am thinking about it all the time, I am already guilty of adultery; you will even invoke the words of Jesus as proof that your logic is sound.

Matthew 5:28 [NIV] But I tell you that anyone who looks at a woman lustfully has already committed adultery with her in his heart.

In my dark, depressed, tormented mind, this is the exact logic I used to rationalize the final steps that took the adultery from imagination to reality. At this point you will be thinking, I may as well go ahead and commit the act, because I am lost anyway. I can't stress strongly enough that you flee from such logic; fight it with everything in you and ask God to help you in destroying such ideas, because that mindset will be the tipping point of your infidelity.

The Actor/Hypocrite

And while there is a vast difference between adultery of the heart and adultery of the body, the issue is that God looks at the heart, and whatever is in the heart will then motivate the behavior.

I have a very good friend, he is an old marine, and one of his favorite sayings is: "They could put me in jail for what I've been thinking about you." That may sound catchy but it is far from the truth. They cannot put you in jail for what you are thinking; you have to commit an act to be put into jail. However, God can and will judge us according to both our thoughts and our actions. And in the end, we will forfeit our birthright and our destiny if we allow sin to reign over us.

Consider this: The devil can never entice us by offering things we consider worthless. That means his tool of choice is to offer us exactly what we think we want. It will enslave us every time.

The sad thing about this scenario is that you have no one to talk to about the affair you are having in your heart/mind. No one other than God, is aware there is a battle raging; remember you're operating in actor/hypocrite mode, never revealing the truth, even to those closest to you.

Because of shame, embarrassment, fear, pride, ego or whatever, you refuse to open up and talk to someone. And that pretty well seals your doom. I have often wished that I had spoken to just one person . . .

Note: Jesus did not design ministry as a one-man show. He was well-aware of the frailty of man. When His disciples were ready to get their feet wet in ministry, note what Jesus did.

YOUR PASTOR NEEDS THIS BOOK

Mark 6:7 [NIV] Calling the twelve to him, he sent them out two by two and gave them authority over evil spirits.

Our modern day Christian church may need to revisit the concept of two by two.

<u>Transparency and accountability with just one other person can keep you on the straight and narrow, in ways nothing else can.</u>

I wish I had mustered the fortitude to sit my wife down, look her in the eyes and say, "I have a problem, I need your help." Hindsight is not worth much, but I know today, without a doubt, that she could have saved me.

A word of advice to you, if you are in the "adultery of the heart" stage of your affair, there is still hope for you. But only if, and that is a big if; if you confess your sin to someone. But you must stop the acting, realizing that everything is not alright, and your boat is sinking.

You must apply biblical principles that were established by the God of creation for one reason, to safeguard those He loves. James did not write chapter five because he had extra ink he needed to use up. He was inspired by God to pen these words:

James 5:16 [NIV] Therefore confess your sins to each other and pray for each other so that you may be healed.

Right about now, confession and repentance are your only hope, so get someone involved in your battle; you are in desperate need of healing; your mind has become diseased. Confession is the beginning of a process that God has established for our survival and restoration. I know it will be tough to do. Believe me

The Actor/Hypocrite

when I say I know this story up close and personal; <u>I was not able to confess my sin, and as a result, I only plunged deeper into a dark pit that I could not escape.</u>

Please read this passage, from the Old Testament book of Malachi. Read it several times to absorb God's clear teaching concerning marriage and divorce. Please do not use the old cop-out that it's the Old Testament. Yes, it is the Old Testament. The Old Testament is the school master that brought us to Christ.

Galatians 3:23-25 [NIV] Before this faith came, we were held prisoners by the law, locked up until faith should be revealed. So the <u>law was put in charge to lead us to Christ</u> that we might be justified by faith. Now that faith has come, we are no longer under the supervision of the law.

The Law of the Old Testament had only one function, to lead us to Christ. The law offers us amazingly detailed glimpses into the nature of God the Father. The Old Testament clearly delineates the loves/hates of the invisible God we strive to please as well as how He thinks. The New Testament, through Jesus Christ, paints us a beautiful picture of the love of God the Father.

I am fully aware and thankful for the fact that we live under New Testament grace as opposed to Old Testament law. But the fact remains that God had never changed His mind about sin, no matter which end of the Bible it's in. The things God hated in the Old Testament, He still hates in the New Testament. The things God loved in the Old Testament, God still loves in the New Testament. The wonderful thing about living in New Testament times is that we can drink from the fountain of God's mercy and grace.

YOUR PASTOR NEEDS THIS BOOK

The folks who lived in Old Testament days were not afforded mercy and grace.

Want proof? I committed a grievous sin against God and I am still alive to tell about it. And what's more I found forgiveness. Had I lived under the law of the Old Testament, the consequences would've been far different.

Deuteronomy 22:22[NIV] If a man is found sleeping with another man's wife, both the man who slept with her and the woman must die. You must purge the evil from Israel.

O.K. now, back to Malachi. This is God's take on marriage and divorce, and it really needs no commentary. I would like for you to read this passage several times.

Malachi 2:14-16 [NLT] You cry out, "Why doesn't the Lord accept my worship?" I'll tell you why! Because the Lord witnessed the vows you and your wife made when you were young.

But you have been unfaithful to her, though she remained your faithful partner, the wife of your marriage vows.

Didn't the Lord make you one with your wife? In body and spirit you are his. And what does he want? Godly children from your union. So guard your heart; remain loyal to the wife of your youth.

 "For I hate divorce!" says the Lord, the God of Israel. "To divorce your wife is to overwhelm her with cruelty," says the Lord of Heaven's Armies. "So guard your heart; do not be unfaithful to your wife."

Note these instructions are given twice, guard your heart.

The wise man of Proverbs gives exactly the same advice.

The Actor/Hypocrite

Proverbs 4:23 [NIV] Above all else, <u>guard your heart</u>, for it is the wellspring of life.

To address the problem of unfaithfulness that starts in the heart we have many scriptural warnings, telling us to guard our hearts. So we must ask ourselves the question: "<u>How can we guard our hearts</u>?"

Should we isolate ourselves from women? Would that safeguard our hearts? It might help, but it's not practical, and neither is it the cure. Is that the reason religious monks advocate isolation? In light of our frail, weak, carnal nature, is it even possible to guard ourselves from the clutches of the enemy and the temptation of lust that wants to enslave us?

Yes, it is possible. I find one particular scripture that shows us how to stave off temptation. This is the only scripture I can find that tells me how my heart can be guarded.

Philippians 4:6 [NIV] Don't worry about anything; instead, pray about everything. Tell God what you need, and thank him for all he has done.
7 Then you will experience God's peace, which exceeds anything we can understand. <u>His peace will guard your hearts and minds</u> as you live in Christ Jesus.
                His PEACE will guard our hearts.

How do we get His peace to set up watch over our hearts/minds? What huge mistake did I make that caused His guarding peace to relinquish guard of my heart?

I have come to the conclusion that God has made it simple for us, as fragile humanity, to walk with Him. So simple in fact that we sometimes overlook or should I say neglect the very things that keep us strong and protected in God.

YOUR PASTOR NEEDS THIS BOOK

If you want a guarded heart, here is the recipe.

1. Don't worry about anything
2. Pray about everything
3. Tell God what you need
4. Thank Him for all He has done
5. Abide in Christ Jesus
6.

Then you will experience God's peace.

As with most great truths in the Word of God, the simplicity will startle you. <u>In order to guard your heart all you have to do is to maintain daily devotions, soaking in His presence, and maintaining a close, passionate walk with Jesus</u>.

Don't worry about anything!
Sure sounds like somebody is out of touch with reality, right? Who says--don't worry about anything? What planet is this guy from? Get real, everyone worries. Surely this scripture is translated incorrectly; no way can it mean what it says. Surely the guy that wrote this didn't have any problems.

The guy who wrote this passage, under the inspiration of the Holy Spirit, did seem to have a problem or two, problems that would make our whining seem embarrassingly small and insignificant.

The writer who penned the line, "<u>Don't worry about anything,</u>" had the following qualifications:

2 Corinthians 11:23-28 [NIV] I have worked much harder, been in prison more frequently, been flogged more severely, and been exposed to death again and again.
Five times I received from the Jews the forty lashes minus one. Three times I was beaten with rods, once I was stoned, three times I was shipwrecked, I spent

The Actor/Hypocrite

a night and a day in the open sea, I have been constantly on the move.

I have been in danger from rivers, in danger from bandits, in danger from my own countrymen, in danger from Gentiles; in danger in the city, in danger in the country, in danger at sea; and in danger from false brothers.

I have labored and toiled and have often gone without sleep; I have known hunger and thirst and have often gone without food; I have been cold and naked. Besides everything else, I face daily the pressure of my concern for all the churches.

Let's see now, the guy who said don't worry was:

- Flogged
- Repeatedly threatened with death
- Five times received thirty-nine lashes
- Three times beaten with rods
- Stoned once
- Shipwrecked three times
- Spent a night and day in the open sea
- Constantly on the move [no home]
- In danger of his countrymen who wanted to kill him
- In danger in the city
- In danger in the country
- In danger from the Gentiles
- In danger from bandits
- Hungry, cold, and tired

Anyone want to volunteer to change places with that guy? I didn't think so.

I think most of us believe there are probably only two types of people in the world who do not worry.

YOUR PASTOR NEEDS THIS BOOK

1. Someone who is mentally challenged

Keep in mind that I mean no disrespect to anyone who is mentally handicapped, but we often hear the phrase; "You'd have to be crazy not to worry about that."

My wife has a mentally handicapped sister who is seventy-seven years old with the mind of a two-year old. When I say she does not have a worry in the world, I mean she literally doesn't have a worry in the world. I do not think she has the capacity to worry. Someone provides everything she needs; she is like a little child.

2. A child

After twenty-nine years without the pitter patter of small feet in our home, we were blessed with our first grandchild. Talk about a change in our life. Oh, the renewed feelings those small feet have caused to resurface from down deep inside me. There is nothing in the world like the love you have for a child-- nothing.

Children have no worries. While at my house, if my grandchild is hungry, I feed him. If he is dirty, I bathe him. If he is sleepy, I put him to bed. If he is crying, I hold him. If he falls, I pick him up. If he skins his knee, I kiss the knee. If he is outside walking, I hover over him like an old mother hen. If he is inside, he is never out of my sight. Trust me, this kid has no worries.

When Paul said, "Don't worry about anything," he had to have an understanding of the concept that God is our Father and He loves us far more than we could ever love our children. With that thought firmly ingrained in our minds we can be fearless, for as scripture says, "Perfect loves casts out fear." However, for some reason this concept seems to elude us as adults. And as long as that happens we will worry.

The Actor/Hypocrite

Matthew 18:3 [NIV] And he said: "I tell you the truth, unless you change and become like little children, you will never enter the kingdom of heaven.

Jesus had to be talking about the trait of faith and confidence that all children share. The faith and confidence that Father is going to make all things right.

The bottom line is this: it's all about relationship with God.

Praying involves meditating and talking to God, as well as thanking and praising God, telling Him what's on your heart, and surrendering the fears that plague you.

The key to being worry-free is intimate time spent in His presence.

The key to survival as a God-called minister is personal devotional time . . . such a simple concept, so important, so vital....yet so often neglected. Answer this question right now and be honest. Do you have your own personal and intimate devotional time where you spend time talking with God?

Did you spend time with the Boss today? How about yesterday? Is there peace in your heart from that daily recharging of the spiritual batteries that makes your inner man strong? Is your heart being guarded? Only you can answer that question, but statistics prove that the majority of preachers reading this right now spend no meaningful time alone with God.

Of 1,050 pastors polled, only 270 or 26 percent said they regularly had personal devotions and felt they were adequately spiritually fed.

YOUR PASTOR NEEDS THIS BOOK

That means 74% of pastors spend no time alone with God!

So what can we conclude from that statistic?
There's clearly a lot of acting going on in the pulpit!!!
To which of these groups do you belong, the 74 percent or the 26 percent?

Seventy percent said the only time they spend studying the Word is when they are preparing their sermons.

I repeat—a lot of acting going on here......

As a pastor, you haven't a snowball's chance in hell of surviving temptation and spiritual ruin if you do not spend time alone with God and meditate on His Word. Sorry guys, but there is no way to circumvent the truth; you will never make it, because there is no guard at the door of your heart.

God put into affect something simple to insure our safety and security--something so simple that we often have difficulty grasping its importance. The result of such negligence is an unguarded heart that will end up simply playing a part.

We will find ourselves putting on an ACT.

The Actor/Hypocrite

This chapter in a nut-shell:

It is impossible to walk with God without personal devotions. Prayer, bible meditations, and quite time with God are the only things that can guard your heart.

Who Will You Have an Affair With

Several years ago I received a call from a gentleman who wanted me to do some work on his home. We set a time for me to go to his house to discuss the project and to get a first-hand look at the scope of work. On the phone he seemed like a very nice guy, well spoken, courteous. I knew by the address that he had given me that he lived in an upscale neighborhood. I had a good feeling about the job.

I showed up for the meeting fifteen minutes early; I hate to be late. I think punctuality is a vital ingredient for success in any business. I am the guy who is always early.

I arrived for my appointment and everything appeared normal. His home was in a very nice subdivision. I easily found his address, and saw a lovely home, with a manicured lawn and beautiful landscaping. There was a new Lincoln in the driveway. I saw all the signs of a successful life before I even got to the door.

When I rang the doorbell, the door opened just enough for the man inside to ask, "Who are you?" I told him who I was, and that I had an appointment to estimate a renovation project. I was beginning to think I was at the wrong address. He asked me, "Do you have a business card for identification?" Needless to say, I was getting a little uneasy. I slipped my business card through the slightly opened door, which I noticed had two safety chains attached, wondering if I should just get into my truck and drive away. Something just wasn't right. He took my business

Who Will You Have An Affair With

card, and then said, "I'll be with you in a moment."
As he closed the door, I could hear him lock the
chains. I was standing outside, no doubt wearing a
confused look on my face, wondering what to do. I
was seriously considering a quick exit. Then the door
swung open, and out stepped a guy about sixty years
old, impeccably dressed. He reached out to shake my
hand wearing a smile that would have made any
politician jealous.

However, at that moment, I was not nearly as focused on his neat, pressed clothing and wide Holly-
wood smile as I was on the Baby Glock tucked into
his starched trousers! Trust me; the gun had all my
attention. This small town country boy had never, in
his fifty years, had someone answer the door with a
gun tucked into his waistband. Maybe in the world
where you live this is normal, but for me, I'm sure I
wore the look of a deer staring at headlights.

All kinds of thoughts raced through my mind. Did this
guy just shoot his wife? Is this guy a psycho with a
gun? I wonder if he's an escapee from the nut-house.
But in all truthfulness, probably the loudest thought
screaming in my mind was--Why the h_ _ _ does this
guy have a gun in his pants?

And yet, Paul turned out to be one of the neatest
guys I have ever met. Because he was all about being
aware of danger and prepared at all times, over the
next few days I received a cram course on personal
security. He was like a preacher with one subject.
We've all crossed paths with this type of person—the
one who steers every conversation in one direction—
in this case toward the need for situational awareness.

My wife was with me one day when I stopped by
Paul's house; it was priceless. The gun-toting,

situational awareness preacher had himself a new sinner to convert. I kid you not; he preached his message to my wife for two hours. I just smiled encouragement.

She heard about the need for mace, otherwise known as pepper spray. He told her where to park when shopping, what to do if you approach your car in a parking lot and see it has a flat tire. She learned of the unpardonable sin, parking beside a van. He told her about the Blue Light Rapist, and then jumped right into the doctrine of serial killers. While standing in his front yard he actually taught her how to knee a man in the groin.

Paul lived by a system that included a code with three levels: yellow, orange, and red. Yellow was inside his home, where there was really nothing to worry about. Orange: applied to anywhere outside his home and required just a little more caution. Red alert included anything out of the ordinary that was perceived as an opportunity for danger.

Most of Paul's doctrine of situational awareness is just good old common sense, things that we know to do, but fail to make a part of our everyday lives.

For example, home invasions: Someone knocks on your door, you open it, he rushes in, puts a gun in your face, and beats you up or kills you, and then loots your home. Ten years ago we had never heard the term "home invasion", but now the statistics of home invasion crime will scare you:

- Thirty-eight percent of assaults and sixty per cent of rapes occur during home invasions
- One in five homes undergoes a home invasion or break-in

Who Will You Have An Affair With

- There are more than 8,000 home invasions every day in North America
- Fifty percent of home invasions involve the use of a weapon; the most common weapons used are knives or other cutting instruments
- In 48 percent of home invasions, victims sustain physical injuries
- Victims age sixty or older make up 17 percent of home invasion victims
- In 68 percent of home invasions, victims and the accused are strangers;
- In 11 percent of these cases, victims and the accused are friends, business associates, or family members.

The deterrent to home invasions is actually very simple. Do not open your door to anyone you do not know. When the doorbell rings train yourself to go into an orange/caution mode.

Now that Paul has made me aware of some very common dangers, you can ring my doorbell until you're blue in the face, but I will not open the door if I don't know you. In response to his suggestions I made a few minor adjustments in my life, and I feel much safer now.

At this point I want to apply Paul's situational awareness system another way:
As a man, you also need to develop an acute awareness in another area-- where you are most vulnerable to the temptation/danger of adultery.

Where and how will that temptation come?

There are some very simple deterrents to adultery that every man, and especially every pastor, should be aware of and should exercise every day of his life; they need to become a way of life.

YOUR PASTOR NEEDS THIS BOOK

As I learned from Paul, if you can identify <u>where you</u> are most likely to be tempted, you can be on guard, exercise caution, and beware of the danger. If you can identify <u>with whom</u> you are most likely to commit adultery, then you will at least have a fighting chance in the battle against the lust of the flesh.

As for whom, you really don't have to worry about the beautiful movie star who catches your eye on television. The famous woman on the cover of the magazine may stir your hormones, but the chances of an affair with her are pretty close to zero. <u>Sorry guys, it just ain't gonna happen.</u> The same goes for the attractive lady who pulls up beside you at a red light. She may cause you to turn and look, but there is not much danger there, because you will probably never see her again. The professional prostitute probably isn't someone you need to worry about. She's certainly not one to cause most ministers to stray from the straight and narrow.

<u>As a rule, statistics indicate that before a man and a woman commit adultery, they will first become friends. They will spend time together and develop a friendship that will eventually lead them down the road where adultery lives.</u>

I am by no means suggesting that there are not some men on the prowl, looking for a woman to jump into bed with at a moments notice. There are definitely men on the make looking to commit adultery.

However, I personally feel those men are a minority. I think most men want to be good husbands and remain faithful to their wives, particularly Christian men. I have always lived my life on the premise that our inherent desire is for righteousness, because God made us that way. It is with this attitude that I address adultery. It is with this view that I see preachers; you do not have adultery on your agenda.

Who Will You Have An Affair With

It is not something that is written in your day planner: "This Monday, make time for an affair."

<u>Adultery is not a "wake up one day and just do it" kind-of thing</u>. It will be a process, a building process that takes time . . . a friendship must be developed, a comfort level reached, and trust established.

This may shock you but it is the truth. You will find yourself doing the same things, acting the same way and saying the same kind things you did when dating your wife, you will find yourself acting the exact same way with the woman with whom you will commit adultery. The only difference is that with your wife, it was all done out in the open. When you begin to walk down the path leading to adultery, everything is done in secret, hiding in darkness.

This process is going to take months. If at any time during this bonding process you can somehow become aware of what is happening, you may be able to call a halt to it and salvage yourself.

In Number 11:20 [NIV] the children of Israel are instructed to take the words of the Lord and,
"Write them on the doorframes of your houses and on your gates." The reason for writing God's words on the doorpost and gates was very simple; the children of Israel would see the writings every time they walked through the door or gate. It would be a daily, constant reminder of what God wanted them to know.

Make a mental note of the statistic I am about to share with you, let it be engraved in the recesses of your mind; commit this statistic to memory, and never forget it.

Engrave into the doorpost of your heart and into the gate of your soul, this fact you are about to read.

YOUR PASTOR NEEDS THIS BOOK

Think about this fact every time you walk into your workplace.

According to statistics, the workplace is the #1 place for married people to meet those with whom they will engage in infidelity.

Bear in mind that statistics on adultery are to be taken with a grain of salt, because <u>those who commit adultery also lie</u>.

> "Oh what a tangled web we weave,
> When first we practice to deceive!"
> Sir Walter Scott

If you were to conduct a survey and ask 1000 people if they prefer chicken or beef, you would probably get 1000 honest answers. But if you ask the same 1000 people, "Have you ever committed adultery?" your results would be suspect. Adulterers do not volunteer information, and when asked if they are committing adultery, they will deny it categorically. <u>I can personally vouch for the truth of this statement</u>.

The adultery numbers are no doubt much higher than the statistics indicate, but no matter what the statistics say, adultery is a sin that never stands alone. The harsh reality is that in order to commit adultery, you must first become a prolific liar. <u>Lying and adultery are Siamese twins;</u> you will always see them together. You lie about where you have been, you lie about where you are going, you lie about who you are talking to, you lie about why you are late, and the list goes on and on.

Having said that, statistics clearly indicate that 60 percent of all affairs begin in the workplace. Another reality can no longer be ignored: as the number of women in the workplace has increased, divorce numbers have also surged.

Who Will You Have An Affair With

Apparently it's impossible to have men and women who are not married to each other, working and being together on a daily basis without temptation.

I must insert here that I am in no way inferring that women should not work. In our society it is almost a necessity that both work outside the home to make ends meet. However, in defense of men, let me also add that they seem to be getting a bad rap for initiating adultery. But let's do the math, if 1000 men are committing adultery, then how many women are committing adultery? It takes two. Enough said.

As late as 1940, less than 12 percent of married women were in the workforce; today the figure is nearly 60 percent.

In 1960, over 70 percent of all American families were made up of a breadwinner father, a stay-at-home mother, and their children. Today, "traditional" families with a working husband and a stay-at-home wife and one or more children make up less than 15 percent of the nation's households.

As men and women were thrown together in the workplace, look what happened--divorce rates soared from 1960 to 1980.

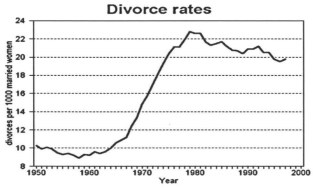

Divorce rates

Source: Monthly Vital Statistics Reports

YOUR PASTOR NEEDS THIS BOOK

The most dangerous place on the planet, when it comes to the lure of adultery, is the workplace.

All Christians, whether men or women, need to go into **RED ALERT** mode every time they walk into the workplace because it is a perfect breeding ground for infidelity. Knowing this fact could mean the difference between, you as a Christian, surviving the workplace infidelity trap or becoming a statistic.

Consider this: you will probably spend more time this week at work, with a man or woman who is not your mate, than you will spend with your husband or wife. **RED ALERT**! Time spent together is where friendships are born.

Today you will probably talk more with someone at work than you will with your husband or wife. **RED ALERT**! Friendship always begins with conversation.
The unavoidable time together at work, spent dealing with the same job challenges, will lead to conversation, which will lead to understanding, which will lead to familiarity, which will ultimately lead to friendship.

You will first discuss work issues, but as the friendship grows, you will move to personal problems . . . **RED ALERT**!

A married man should have no place in his life for women friends; it is the recipe for disaster.

When a married man or married woman says, "Oh, she/he is just a friend," your mind should flash: **RED ALERT**!

Here is a pretty good test to see if you are building a dangerous relationship with a woman at your workplace. Do you freely talk about the "friend" at home with your wife; do you call her by name? Do you tell

Who Will You Have An Affair With

your wife what you and your "friend" talk about? If, at home, you are hiding, keeping mum about your friendship with your new-found friend, chances are, you are cultivating a garden that will yield a crop you will regret planting.

People who have committed adultery will often say, "It just happened. I didn't plan on committing adultery." But as one who has walked the sordid path to adultery, <u>let me interpret that statement</u>.

In the early stages of what will end up in adultery, a friendship is being cultivated. As the relationship develops everything you're doing is perfectly normal, which is why people can't explain what happened to them or why it happened. Hence the statement, "It just happened." I beg to differ.

It did not just happen!

"We just began talking." What's wrong with talking? "We became friends." What's wrong with friendship? "We took breaks together." What is wrong with taking breaks together? "We sat together during lunch." What is wrong with having lunch together?

During this process, there is no outward sin that you can put your finger on; there is just a man and a woman building a friendship. But inside, something is brewing. It happens so gradually that you will probably not be able to recognize it for what it is, the deadly sin of lust. The undeniable truth is that friendship is dangerous, with the opposite sex.

<u>Pastor</u>, friendship with any woman other than your wife should scream **RED ALERT**! "This is not right, this is dangerous, and this is crossing the line of ethics."

YOUR PASTOR NEEDS THIS BOOK

For the pastor, his workplace is the congregation where he ministers. Like it or not, the reality is this, if you fall into adultery it will probably be with someone in your workplace, your congregation. As terrible as this may sound, it's reality. Right now you may be thinking, "No way, not me . . ." I would have felt the same way if someone had suggested that I would succumb to adultery with a parishioner, <u>but I did</u>.

It seems almost ironic that we would refer to our congregation, our parishioners, as those with whom we must be on **RED ALERT**! But in reality, it is with this group of people, your congregation, women included, that you will spend most of your time.

You preach to them every Sunday, you baptize them and their children, you are around them at social functions; you officiate over their weddings and funerals. You visit them in the hospital, you listen to their problems, and the list goes on and on. There is a bond that is formed between minister and parishioner; a friendship can very easily flourish given that much interaction.

Then on the other hand, you cannot neglect your calling and your service to the congregation. Talk about a two-edged sword.

Is there a solution? If so, what is it?

I learned from my personal situational awareness guru, Paul, that knowledge is the key to survival and the avoidance of danger.

Knowledge: Consider this to be your workplace preparedness class, this class will teach you the need for a Red Alert system. This class will also teach you two things you need to do that will help you survive and remain standing where others have fallen.

Who Will You Have An Affair With

1. Teach the congregation . . .
2. Set boundaries . . . and do not cross them—ever.

Knowledge

I think the greatest deterrent you have in your arsenal for defense is knowledge and this system that includes a **RED ALERT**.

In my twenty years of preaching I attended many events geared toward preparing us as ministers to save the world. Seminars, camp meetings, conferences, retreats, etc. But I have never attended any type of event that even hinted at the subject of preacher fatalities. That needs to change. Instead of every event centering on saving the world, someone needs to host events to "save the pastor."

Just knowing where the greatest danger lies for you, as a pastor, will go a long way to help you protect yourself. In the back of your mind, let the thought always be, this is my workplace. I am subject to error here, so I must be vigilant.

Teach the Congregation

Every church has business meetings several times a year. I think this would be a wonderful opportunity to discuss something other than just the church budget. Address the subject of Pastor Fatality. Let the congregation know about dos and don'ts associated with interaction with their pastor.

"Fifteen hundred pastors leave the ministry each month due to moral failure, spiritual burnout, or contention in their churches."
FASICLD (Francis A. Schaeffer Institute of Church Leadership Development).

So you might introduce this topic--What can we, as a congregation, do to keep our pastor from becoming a statistic? With the pastor fatality rate as high as it is, it is apparent that some things need to change in regard to the ministry.

<u>Some drastic changes need to be made regarding what we consider ministerial duties and what we do not.</u> And though it goes beyond the scope of this writing to delve into that subject I can assure you that if changes don't occur in this area, neither will the statistics change.

"If you do what you've always done, you'll get what you've always gotten." Anthony Robbins

Another idea you might want to implement: bring in a special speaker qualified to address the subject of pastor responsibilities. The flock really does need to know something about the scope of the pastor's duties. This would be a great time to introduce some guidelines and boundaries.

How about writing a church membership handbook? It could be a hand-out given to every church member, and could cover a variety of topics. One chapter could be devoted to the pastor, perhaps titling it: "Our pastor's duties, responsibilities, and boundaries."

As a pastor, you can spend so much time trying to establish the aura of spirituality that your people may be blinded to the fact that you are also a man with the same carnal nature they have.

Set Boundaries....
I am going to mention one boundary.

First and foremost, before all other boundaries is rule #1! The most important rule of all!

No doubt you've seen these warning signs:
- Danger ahead!

Who Will You Have An Affair With

- Do not cross this line!
- Detour--bridge out!
- Caution--dangerous animals!
- Hazardous materials!
- RR crossing ahead!
- Beware of dog!

Every warning and caution sign combined cannot overemphasize the importance of, or the danger of violating what I will call "boundary number one."

Absolutely no one-on-one counseling!!

Taking that concept one step further, I would avoid any one-on-one conversation with women period, case closed, no deviation allowed, boundary set. You might be thinking right about now, that is just not possible, or, that idea is just too old-school, or, "Come on, this is the twenty first century."

Here is old school in black and white.

2 Timothy 2:22 [NLT] <u>Run from anything that stimulates youthful lusts.</u> Instead, pursue righteous living, faithfulness, love, and peace. Enjoy the companionship of those who call on the Lord with pure hearts.

Run from anything that stim-u-lates; to excite (a nerve, gland, etc.) to its functional activity.

Being alone with a woman stimulates a man, period, no explanation needed.

I betcha one thing, if I was ever in the pastoring business again [I never will be] you would <u>NEVER</u> and I say <u>NEVER</u>, do you hear me, <u>NEVER</u>, put myself into a position where I am alone with any woman other than my wife. And let me reiterate that I would even avoid isolated one-on-one conversations with women.

YOUR PASTOR NEEDS THIS BOOK

I set this as a personal boundary; years ago I made it a rule to avoid being with or talking to any woman alone. Of course, that was after I broke the seventh commandment, at a time in my life <u>when I was not even walking with God</u>. If I had set this boundary when I was a pastor, my life may not have detoured down the path that leads to adultery.

What I am writing about is not just a preacher thing, it is a man thing. I am addressing concepts that will help any man, believer or not, to avoid the problem of flesh overpowering the common sense of duty.

My work sometimes requires me to travel. I was going to be working about 200 miles from home on one particular building project that would take five months to complete. I would be on the jobsite Tuesday, Wednesday and Thursday of each week.

There are two things in life that I do not enjoy: one, staying in motels, two, eating out. I like to sleep in my bed, and I love to cook.

To add to my disdain for motels, the Oprah show did a segment on motels that would make anyone cringe. On the show they ran an ultraviolet light across the bedspread that would expose body fluids that the naked eye could not see. Let me just say that I have not lain on a motel bedspread since that show. The very first thing I do in a motel is take two fingers and remove the bedspread from the bed, then go wash my hands.

And lest you believe otherwise the motels where they tested the spreads were not just low-end dives. Motels, whether high end or low, just do not wash bedspreads daily as they do sheets.

As for eating out, after seeing the "Dirty Dozen," you just have to wonder if the chips you are eating were

Who Will You Have An Affair With

on another table before they were served hot and fresh to you. And the salsa and refried beans are also easy to recycle and re-serve.

To avoid the motel and restaurant scene while working this job, I decided to search on Craigslist for a bedroom in a private home to rent/lease. I found the perfect place, a bedroom downstairs with a private bathroom, and I could use the kitchen as much as I wanted. The husband and wife lived alone, after their children were grown and off to college. The neighborhood was nice, and like many people today, the couple needed some additional income.

They liked me, and I liked them. When they found out I enjoyed cooking they jokingly said, "We will give you the room at no charge, if you will cook for us. We never cook." They were ready to commit the room to me for four months.

Up to that point the nice couple had been asking all the questions, but before I handed them the non-refundable $2000 they required for four months rent in advance, I had a couple of questions to ask.

In the end, I stayed at a motel and ate restaurant food. The husband traveled some with his job and the wife did not work, which meant she was at home alone all day. It was a deal breaker because years earlier I had drawn a personal boundary line that I will never again cross.

Here's something to think about: you can stand in a church sanctuary with 400 people milling around, and engage in inappropriate conversation with a woman. I know that to be a fact because <u>I did just that with the other woman in my life.</u> This is often referred to as hiding in plain sight. People can be in plain view, but out of hearing range. The power of assumption kicks in; they just assume the conversation is innocent.

YOUR PASTOR NEEDS THIS BOOK

You can flirt and carry on like school kids and unless others overhear the conversation, they are none the wiser.

I now live by a very simple policy. If my wife cannot stand beside me and listen, I do not need to be talking to you.

Most pastors live by what I call the open office door policy. The policy is very simple, if you are talking to a woman in your office, you leave the office door open. It is a wonderful policy, but . . . it doesn't work.

Your adultery will start with conversation, so make a mental note of that fact. With that in mind, it is senseless to think that an open office door is a deterrent; in fact, it's a joke. True, the open door policy will hinder touching, but words will initially fan the flame.

It is conversation that will be the forerunner of physical contact. Of the two, conversation and touch, it is my opinion that conversation holds the most venom. Also, be aware of the fact that your phone may very well become a tool that you use for feeding the lust of your flesh. If you find yourself looking for trivial reasons to call, just to chat with, a particular woman parishioner, you are walking on some very dangerous terrain. During an affair, you will spend much more time on the phone with your new found friend, then you will in person.

If you are wondering if you are on the road to an adulterous relationship, all you have to do is scan your last month phone record. Your phone statistics may preach to you a message you do not want to hear. There is NO reason under God's blue sky for you to call the same woman, who is not your wife, day after day. If you do, you are having an affair; even if it is just in your heart, at this time.

Who Will You Have An Affair With

The open door policy swings both ways; anyone coming by the office can glance in and see you and the person you are talking to, but you are also on the lookout for others coming by. [Smile] Been there, done that.

God enacted a law in the Old Testament; it took a minimum of two witnesses, preferably more, to establish something as fact. It is a very good common-sense law. It may just save your hide someday, if you allow it to become a part of your lifestyle and work ethic.

Deuteronomy 17:6 [NIV] <u>On the testimony of two or three witnesses a man shall be put to death, but no one shall be put to death on the testimony of only one witness.</u>

For the sake of argument let's say you're in your office, offering counsel to someone. Tempers flare, and words are said in anger; things quickly escalate out of control. Charges are brought against you; you are called before the church board, or even worse, a court of law. What happened in your office becomes a, he said/I said argument. There are two stories being told, yours and that of the other person. So in this scenario, it becomes your word against their word. Nothing can be proven.

If you make it your policy to have someone sit in on your counseling sessions, there is another set of eyes that see, and another set of ears that hear, protecting your interests. The additional witness also serves as a safeguard for you as pastor, especially if you happen to be going through a tough time spiritually, feeling particularly vulnerable for some reason. Regardless of your state of mind or spirit at the time, the second witness is a wise safeguard and will protect you.

YOUR PASTOR NEEDS THIS BOOK

This is what Paul was telling Timothy; it takes at least two witnesses to make any case. Paul was using the principle established in the Old Testament, that it takes two.

1 Timothy 5:19 [NIV] Do not entertain an accusation against an elder unless it is brought by two or three witnesses.

Back in the early days of ministry they traveled in pairs, apparently aware of something we aren't. Because there is safety in numbers, we should attempt to never be alone in ministry. "Let not then your good be evil spoken of."

Forget the open door policy; get another pair of eyes and ears involved, and have no private conversations with women.

You might want to record all conversations or use security cameras throughout the church. They are not expensive and are a good safeguard. But the bottom line is this; recorders can be turned off, security cameras also. An extra set of eyes and ears are without doubt the safest security program.

I hope by now the, "where", and the, "with whom", questions have been answered, forever engraved on your mind and in your heart.

It is my prayer that you will always be on **Red Alert** as you minister to the congregation God has called you to lead.

Who Will You Have An Affair With

This chapter in a nut-shell:

If you have an affair it will probably be with someone in your congregation. Avoid being alone with women. Affairs start with conversation.

Go, Show Yourself to the Priest

Jesus reached out his hand and touched the man. "I am willing," he said. "Be clean!" Immediately he was cured of his leprosy. 4 Jesus said to him, "See that you don't tell anyone. <u>But go, show yourself to the priest</u> and offer the gift Moses commanded, as a testimony to them." Matthew 8:3-4 [NIV]

One of the great things about the Word of God is that if you have a question, it has probably already been addressed in its pages. You may have to dig, search, study, and pray to find it, but the answer to any and all of life's questions can be found somewhere between Genesis and Revelations.

Many times, after you discover the answer in His Word, you will shake your head and wonder, why didn't I see that before? You may have read a particular passage a hundred times, and then an answer just leaps off the page. We refer to this as God speaking to us through His Word. That is exactly what happened to me in regard to the Bible teachings concerning sickness and healing.

Like it or not, it is the responsibility of the clergy to minister and offer support to the sick and injured. Praying for the sick and visiting hospitals and nursing homes is a huge part of Christian ministry.

Many who were attracted to Jesus during His three years of ministry had health problems. While it's true that Jesus came to seek and to save what was lost, (see Luke 19:10), and His chief concern was the salvation of lost souls, he was not blind to the sickness and suffering of their physical bodies. He was not, as we sometimes say, so heavenly-minded that He was no earthly good.

I found out early on in my church planting endeavor that it doesn't matter how hard or calloused a person may have been before the onset of illness, if someone comes to pray for his sick loved one, he is usually viewed as a friend of the family forever. I made many friends and won entire families to God simply because I was there to pray in their times of sickness.

I am sure this has not changed in the past twenty years; sickness often creates a need and softens a previously unreceptive heart. A soft heart is a fertile field in which to plant the seed of the love of God. Sickness may serve as the germinal stage for a personal relationship with Jesus.

Brother James tells us that if any one is sick, he should call for the elders of the church to pray over him.

James 5:14[NIV] Is any one of you sick? He should call the elders of the church to pray over him and anoint him with oil in the name of the Lord.

This is the New Testament doctrine concerning prayer for the sick. Very few, if any Christians use this formula anymore.

1. Call the elders of the church
2. The elders come to your house
3. The elders pray
4. The elders anoint with oil
5. The rest is up to God

Not to rock the boat, but in the New Testament there is no mention or even an inference of a monarchical episcopacy or single leader in the Church.

YOUR PASTOR NEEDS THIS BOOK

Under the New Testament church structure, if you became sick, you didn't call the pastor; you called the elders.

To put this into perspective or to see the faith involved in asking for prayer, we must reset our religious minds to another era of time; the era of the New Testament Church. The church era of which it was said (in Acts 17:6 ESV): "These men who have turned the world upside down have come here also." Wouldn't we love to have that as our testimony today!

It is hard for us to imagine a time of no automobiles, and no phones much less cell phones, primitive doctors, no hospitals or dentists, no eyeglasses, few drugs for pain, and few medicines to promote healing. Back then it was in your best interest to avoid sickness if at all possible. If you can wrap your mind around all that, you might be able to see the tremendous fear of sickness that had reigned until the time of Jesus. If you were sick, there just wasn't much hope. You would simply stay sick until you died or until the sickness ran its course and you recovered.

It was onto that stage, with this backdrop of human suffering and sickness, where the Son of God began to heal all manner of sickness and disease.

Is it any wonder that the multitudes followed Jesus into the desert, traveled from far distant cities, pressed through mob-like crowds, and even endured verbal abuse, just to touch His garment in the hope of being healed? For the first time in their lives they felt there was hope, and they realized that the hope that was rising up in them was Jesus Christ.

If you and I had lived in that dispensation deprived of medical ingenuity, and if we were sick and suffering, or if our loved one was sick and suffering, we would have been among those in the crowds, pressing to touch Jesus.

On their first commission, the twelve were instructed by the Master to heal the sick, according to Matthew 10:1, He called his twelve disciples to him and gave them authority to drive out evil spirits and to heal every disease and sickness.

Then Jesus sent out the seventy-two, two by two, telling them, "When you enter into a town, heal the sick that are there." Luke 10:8-9 [NIV]

Jesus spent much of His ministry praying for the sick and healing all manner of sickness and disease.

When John the Baptist was cast into prison, his faith was apparently wavering a bit. Well, "wavering a bit" may be an understatement, especially if you, like John, are questioning whether Jesus is the Messiah. At this place, you are at the bottom of the barrel of faith, the barrel is empty. John the Baptist was out of faith; his barrel was empty.

John sent two of his disciples to find Jesus and ask Him one question—the only thing John wanted to know, "Are you the one who was to come, or should we expect someone else?" This was the same John who, when he saw the Spirit decent upon Jesus at His baptism, declared, "Behold the lamb of God that takes away the sins of the world."

It is amazing how situations in life can cause a person to question a momentous, even profound occasion that happened in his life. At that point John is no longer on the banks of the Jordan River baptizing people, he is in a jail cell awaiting his execution for remarks he made about Herod's wife and adultery.

YOUR PASTOR NEEDS THIS BOOK

That is the frame of mind in which John finds himself. He is questioning the day he saw the Spirit descend upon Jesus. John is questioning his pronouncement of the Christ. John is wondering, is Jesus really the Messiah? We have all been there and done that, questioned something we believed and stood firm on until the day circumstances changed in our lives, usually for the worst.

In the sunlight of God's blessing and mercy, it is very easy to maintain an unshakeable faith. But let the sunlight fade into dark clouds of tragedy and defeat, and you will find the faith song much harder to sing with conviction and feeling. At that point the sunlight had vanished from John's life and ministry, and he found himself in the darkest hour of his life.

Jesus told John's disciples, "Go back and report to John what you have seen and heard: The blind receive sight, the lame walk, those who have leprosy are cured, the deaf hear, the dead are raised, and the good news is preached to the poor." Jesus could have very easily answered his cousin, John, with a simple yes or no, but He didn't. John knew that when the Christ appeared, a new era was going to begin--an era where sick people would be prayed over and be healed.

Healing of the sick was to be one of the unmistakable signs that the Christ had arrived. Jesus knew that John was well aware of the signs that would introduce the Christ, thus, Jesus' answer was far more effective than a simple yes or no.

After the death, burial and resurrection of Jesus, the healing continued, as recorded in Acts 3, where Peter and John went to the temple to pray, ultimately healing the cripple. In Acts 9, a blind Saul of Tarsus was also healed. He had been a powerful opponent of Jesus as the Messiah, until the stunning experience on the road to Damascus. It was a sickness [Paul had been blinded] and a healing that transformed Paul's opinion as well as his heart.

Healing so permeated the New Testament that anyone, even a non-believer, who begins to read the Bible would have to be obtuse not to understand that healing is a vital part of the Christian faith/doctrine. Healing is one of the central themes woven through out the pages of the New Testament from Matthew to Revelation; I cannot fathom anyone failing to grasp this point.

Jesus began His earthly ministry in Matthew 4 [NIV], "by teaching in their synagogues, preaching the good news of the kingdom, and healing every sickness and disease among the people."

In Revelations, at the completion of all things, John describes a place where, "He, God, will wipe every tear from their eyes. There will be no more death or mourning or crying or pain." Heaven is a place where no sickness is allowed, and there is no need for healing.

But until that day arrives, many questions and problems arise regarding praying for the sick. They are tough questions--questions which tend to put the clergy on the defensive.

1. Call the elders of the church
2. The elders come to your house
3. The elders pray
4. The elders anoint with oil
5. The rest is up to God

Call the elders of the church:
Just imagine you are living in the days of the early church; it is midnight, and you begin to sweat profusely, with knife-like pain in your side. You begin to

retch with dry heaves, while fading in and out of consciousness. You are concerned for your life. You cannot dial 9-1-1, expecting help to arrive within minutes. We teach our children at a very early age to dial 9-1-1 for help. It would be foolish not to use every source available to them in a time of emergency. Because there was no other source of help, the early church taught people to call for the elders of the church.

There were no phones. No quick calls to get the church elders to the house of the sick. There were no automobiles. No quick trip to pick up the elders. Someone had to be sent to the home of the elders, knock on their doors, tell them the need for prayer and then wait for the elder to get dressed, before the long walk back to the house of the sick person, even in pitch darkness of night.

I do not know how many elders were contacted, but I assume there were several, and that they lived in different parts of the city.

The picture I am trying to paint here is the picture that calling for the elders of the church for prayer was a very serious and time-consuming endeavor. It is possible that hours would have passed before they joined in prayer. Calling for the elders, was a tremendous act of faith; it was done in obedience to a biblical principle, and apparently the results were worth whatever effort was required. I am sure that the sick person and his family, anxiously awaited the arrival of the elders. I must say that during that painfully long wait, all minds were probably in agreement in faith, expecting a healing to occur because of the obedience to the Word of God.

<u>In sickness, have you ever called for the elders of the church?</u>

Go, Show Yourself To The Priest

The elders come to your house:
The elders were gathering in your home. Prayer was going to be offered in your home. When is the last time that you heard prayers being prayed in your home?

- When is the last time your wife heard you pray?
- When is the last time your husband heard you pray?
- But more importantly, when is the last time your children heard their parents pray in the home?

The Elders Come to Pray:
The elders were not coming to dinner, they were not coming to watch a movie; they were not coming to play a game, or for social reasons, the elders were coming to pray.

You see, it is possible that without saying a word we can set precedence of what is acceptable and what is unacceptable. <u>Our silence in prayer, in our home, preaches the silent doctrine that prayer is not acceptable at home. You never have to say a word to indoctrinate this belief into your children. All you have to do is be silent on the subject of prayer.</u>

Is it my imagination or has something so stealthy occurred right under our noses of which we are unaware? Has prayer been removed from the home and relegated, as a whole, to the four walls of a church building? I am not talking about prayer in the terms of saying grace at dinner, or kneeling beside your child's bed at night and saying, "Now I lay me down to sleep." I refer to that serious, heartfelt prayer that moves heaven—the kind from the soul that now seems to be confined to our church walls.

YOUR PASTOR NEEDS THIS BOOK

I suppose the argument could be made that the reason the early church members prayed in their homes was because at that time they did not have an actual church building.

But I think the real argument is the fact that the early Christians had a completely different concept concerning prayer. To them prayer was very personal, very real. It was an individual's privilege to approach the throne of God. We must remember, up to the time of Christ, these people had taken sacrifices to a priest, and the priest took the sacrifice and offered it to the Lord. It was the priest that went into the Holy Place, the presence of God. Up to that point only the priest could commune with God in the holy of holies.

Let us be careful lest we revert back to a religious system that silences our prayers and teaches us to bow our heads while another talks to God.

Much is being said about prayer in schools, and I can see the concern on that battlefront, but my concern is not as much for prayer-less schools, as it is for prayer-less homes. There is nothing, except our own lack of purpose to keep us from praying in our homes. God help us to restore prayer back to our homes as those who call ourselves Jesus' disciples.

My wife is the youngest of eleven children. When I married into her family, her dad wasn't just my father-in-law, but he became my best friend. I enjoyed nothing more than sitting with him on his front porch and listening to his stories. He raised his family by trapping alligators in the lake swamps of Louisiana. Before he was married, during the Great Depression he hoboed, as he called it, all across the United States, complements of the railroad. Oh, the stories he had to tell.

Go, Show Yourself To The Priest

He was a big man, six feet four inches tall, and 240 pounds at his prime. When he would take his shirt off, you could see that he bore on his body the marks of a previous life before he knew Jesus. He would never talk about the marks that were obviously made by knives and bullets. He would simply say, "That happened before I met Jesus."

But no story fascinated me more than what I saw with my own two eyes.

It was like I had stepped back in time to another era--a time when people prayed at home. If there was a sickness, they prayed. If there was a problem they prayed. If they were taking a trip, they prayed. If they were coming home from a trip, they prayed. If they were going to bed, they prayed. If they were getting up, they prayed. You did not get much sleep if you stayed overnight in their home because you could hear my mother-in-law and father-in-law praying throughout the night.

That had to be what Paul meant when he said in 1 Thessalonians 5:17 [ESV] "Pray without ceasing."

I was amazed at the people who would come to my father-in-law's house for prayer. They didn't necessarily come because they had a need. They simply came to pray. I was even more amazed at the people who would call, asking him to come and pray for them. He had a few old friends whom he would drive by and pick up when he was called to go to someone's home to pray. I used to wonder sometimes, as close as we were, why he never invited me to go with him to a home for prayer.
But now I understand why--he didn't view me as an elder. He felt he was fulfilling a scriptural command by inviting only elders, and he was right.

YOUR PASTOR NEEDS THIS BOOK

In my father-in-law's late sixties he developed diabetes. Because he had always been a very healthy man his visits to the doctor's office were extremely rare. He only discovered that he was a diabetic, after he stepped on a nail that went into his left shoe and into his big toe. Because he had no feeling in that foot he was completely unaware it had pierced clear through to his toe nail.

The doctor did everything he possibly could to prevent infection, but in time it was clear that he would lose the toe, and possibly even his foot and lower leg to the knee. The hard-headed old man refused to return to the doctor, reasoning that if the doctor said he had done all he could, why waste the man's time? My father-in-law had no intention of letting the doctor amputate any part of his body.

The doctor knew of the faith of my in-laws. Years later when the doctor spoke, at the funeral of my mother–in-law, he said he had become her student, in the things of Christ. He told of how he looked forward to her office visits, because she preached to him about Jesus. He said, "She never called me doctor--it was always brother."

The doctor, who did not make house calls, made a rare home visit, out of concern and respect, to check on my suffering father-in-law. After examining the infected toe/foot/leg, he told the siblings that if they did not get their father to a hospital to have his leg removed just below the knee; their dad was going to die. The doctor made no bones about it; it was amputation or death.

Everyone agreed that we had to talk some sense into his old head. The siblings all agreed that if he would listen to anyone, it would be me. We were very close. It was a very tough assignment; I had to go into the bedroom where he had been lying for weeks, unable

Go, Show Yourself To The Priest

to walk, and convince him to allow a doctor to amputate a part of his leg. It was a huge responsibility.

First and foremost, out of respect for my father-in-law's great faith, I did not want to say anything that would weaken his faith in the healing power of God. But on the other hand, somewhere faith and common sense must come together for the benefit of all involved. I remember thinking, if the old hard-headed guy would just listen to reason...

I well remember walking into his bedroom; I had not seen him in several weeks. He had lost a lot of weight, and his hair was disheveled. He hadn't shaved in several days, and by then his snow white beard was very long and ragged. When he pushed himself up on one elbow to see who was in the room, I could see the pain in his eyes.

For some reason, when I walked into his room and saw the disheveled white hair and the unshaven white beard, I thought, have I stepped back in time? Am I looking at my father-in-law or one of the Old Testament patriarchs? He would have been just as much at home in a sheepskin tent as he was in his king-sized bed.

We had a word of prayer and then I gave it my best shot using all the wisdom and diplomacy I could muster. Choosing my words with care, I explained to the best of my ability the blessing of modern medicine and the wonderful training of doctors. He said nothing; he just lay there for what seemed like forever and I remember thinking, perhaps I actually got through to him just how serious his condition is.
All of a sudden he leaned up on one elbow and looked right into my eyes. With his other hand he jerked the bed sheet that was covering his infected foot, revealing the black and green, infected white skin. I just about lost my breakfast. Up to that time the bed

sheet had masked the awful odor. With fire in his eyes and a certainty in his voice, he told me to go and tell everyone waiting in the hall that he would walk again on that foot, and he nodded his head toward the infected, smelly, rotting flesh.

I simply said, "Yes sir, I will." I must be honest; there was no faith in my heart that what he had just said would ever happen. I told the siblings exactly what he told me. I also told them that regardless of their decision I would not return to try to change his mind.

Suffice it to say that when my father-in-law died years later he still had both of his feet and all of his toes.

<u>I find myself missing the days when the elders prayed in homes.</u>

One of the interesting things about the preaching business is that you never know what the next day or the next phone call will bring. When you think you've seen and heard it all, someone throws you a curve ball you didn't see coming.

One day I was sitting in my office, and a call came from a relatively new convert. She said she needed to meet with me ASAP, to ask my opinion on a very important matter. I didn't see this curve ball coming.

I said, "How about right now? I'm in my church office, and I have a little free time." When she walked into my office she wore a big beautiful smile on her face, which is always a good sign, especially when you are expecting some type of tragedy. We had a word of prayer and then I put on my best, 'how can I help you today face' and waited to hear what the emergency was.

Go, Show Yourself To The Priest

She was a very educated woman, way above me in regard to the number of plaques on her wall. As for walking with Jesus, she had begun that journey about two years earlier. The sad thing about this precious person was the fact that she was in very bad health. Her health problem required her to religiously take medication; some of it was very strong and had very unpleasant side effects.

She had been listening to the radio that very morning, when the preacher on the radio preached about faith in God and His power to heal. Then the radio preacher said, "Someone listening to my voice is being healed right now." She looked me straight in the eyes and said, "Pastor, that was me that God healed."

Well, thus far it had been a great morning, a newer convert giving a wonderful testimony about the power of God. Then came the curve ball, out of nowhere and as usual—unexpected. She said, "I am going to stop taking my medication. I'm healed, so I don't need it."
I look at my wife, who was in the office with us, and my wife looked at me. This woman had brought all her medicine with the full intention of flushing every pill in the ladies bathroom. Furthermore, she was expecting my blessing upon her decision.

It's amazing how many people think that the pastor is suppose to have all the answers; like we actually have a red phone with a direct line to God. This may come as a shock to some of you, but we walk with God in exactly the same way you do, by faith. Faith is not something that is always black and white, something you can easily see. It is the substance of things hoped for, the evidence of things not seen, according to Hebrews 11 [KJV].

YOUR PASTOR NEEDS THIS BOOK

I did not want to rain on her faith in the power of God. But neither did I want her to flush her medication down the ladies' toilet.

And then it came to me, out of nowhere--the story of Jesus healing the leper. It was one of those epiphany moments, when you know God just put a thought into your mind. You know He's spoken to your heart. You find yourself understanding something that just moments ago caused panic in your heart. Oh, the confidence that accompanies experiences like that. It is faith-building to say the least.

A person's faith can be a very fragile thing, like dainty, expensive china, and it should always be handled with extreme care. The wrong words or perceived attitude can destroy a Christian's confidence in the ability of God. I didn't want to say anything that would cause her to doubt the power of God.

So I was walking softly and speaking slowly. We read the passage about Jesus healing the leper, but that was just part of the story. Jesus was the Son of God; He knew that He had healed the leper. But in spite of who He was, and in spite of what He knew to be a fact, there was proper protocol to follow in the healing of leprosy.

<u>Jesus knew, according to the law, He did not have the qualifications needed to tell the man that he was healed.</u>

Jesus had no ego problem when it came to accepting what He was qualified to do and what He was not qualified to do. If the Son of God, could look at someone He had just cleansed of leprosy, and say, "Sorry sir, I am not qualified to pronounce you healed," don't you think we should take His example to heart and gracefully bow out of situations that we are not properly equipped to handle? Make a mental note of this fact as you go about your duties as pastor, living by and working within your qualifications, and it will save you much heartache, grief, and unnecessary work.

I was very happy [and very relieved] to tell this dear parishioner that I was not qualified to declare her healed, but I did know someone who was qualified. If you do not have the answer it is nice to know someone who does. It's called a referral, and it is frequently used in the professional world.

The reason Jesus referred the leper to the priest is found in Leviticus Chapters 13 and 14, where you'll find some interesting and detailed reading. In a nutshell this is the story:

Israel had been enslaved in Egypt for 400 years, when God by His mighty hand, set His people free from the heavy hand of Pharaoh. Then God led Israel through the wilderness with the intention of giving them the land of Canaan as an inheritance. With 600,000 men who were between twenty and sixty years old it is estimated that when Exodus 12:37 was recorded, there could have been anywhere from 2 to 4 million Israelites in the wilderness.

God was going to take this crowd and turn them into a nation. God is going to build a nation out of a group of people who have been doing nothing but gathering straw and making bricks for years and years. If a group of people are going to be converted into a nation, there are a few things they will need to survive as a nation.

Essentials for a new nation to survive:

•   An army, Israel didn't have one.

YOUR PASTOR NEEDS THIS BOOK

- Generals to lead the army, and Israel didn't have any.
- Leaders, Israel didn't have any.
- Laws, Israel didn't have any.
- Lawyers, Israel didn't have any.
- Judges, Israel didn't have any.
- A Church, Israel didn't have any.
- Priests, Israel didn't have any.
- School teachers, Israel didn't have any.
- Physicians, Israel didn't have any.

There were plenty of job openings, in the new nation, but there were none with degrees or training qualified to fill the positions. For the number one spot, President of Israel, God appointed Moses. Moses immediately thought the position was out of his league. Moses pointed this out several times to God.

Exodus 3:11 [NIV] But Moses said to God, "Who am I that I should go to Pharaoh and bring the Israelites out of Egypt?"

Exodus 4:10[NIV] Moses said to the Lord, "O Lord, I have never been eloquent, neither in the past nor since you have spoken to your servant. I am slow of speech and tongue."

Though Moses was once a member of the ruling house of Egypt, that had been years earlier. For the past forty years he had been working as a lowly shepherd. He was now an eighty-year-old man, already past the average life span of his generation.

Basically Moses was telling God: "Look Lord, I'm an eighty-year old shepherd who can't speak."

If Moses was alive today his qualifications would certainly keep him off the ballot for election as President of Israel. But at that point, with or without the paperwork, he would have to fill the position, like it or not.

God also needed someone to head the infectious skin disease diagnostics department; God didn't want to take the chance of an infectious disease spreading throughout the camp. This is what Leviticus 13 and 14 is all about, God instructing Aaron and his sons in regard to the new concept of priesthood; they were instructed on the symptoms of infectious skin diseases. It became their role, because no one else knew what to look for.

The priest duties regarding leprosy:

The priest examines people.

Leviticus 13:3[NIV] "When the priest examines him, he shall pronounce him ceremonially unclean."

The priest had the authority to put people in isolation.

Leviticus 13:4 [NIV] "The priest is to put the infected person in isolation for seven days."

The priest did a reexamination after seven days,

Leviticus 13:5 [NIV] "On the seventh day the priest is to examine him."

If things had not changed after seven days, isolation was the order of the day.

Leviticus 13:5 [NIV] "And if he sees that the sore is unchanged and has not spread in the skin, he is to keep him in isolation another seven days."

There sure are a lot of medical terms used in this passage: examination, isolation, and re-examination.

YOUR PASTOR NEEDS THIS BOOK

This process goes on and on until it is determined whether the person has leprosy or not. The priest were given this job and schooled in what to look for-- the reason? <u>There were no qualified doctors in Israel</u>. After years and years of looking at leprosy, by the time Jesus was born, no one knew leprosy better than the priests.

Today, if you have leprosy or any other disease, you would not go to a priest; you would go to a doctor. With the advances in medicine and the increased knowledge of the human anatomy, there is a special-ist for most any disease you can think of.

The priest no longer examines or re-examines people. Neither does the priest place people into isolation; these are all things that a qualified, licensed medical doctor does. <u>The priest no longer declares clean or unclean, healed or not healed, the physician does</u>.

Back in that day, going to the priest to be examined for leprosy was the only way the leper would ever be able to ever stand and testify, as a fact, that Jesus had healed him. No one was going to argue with the decision of the priest, they were the authority. They were the experts. The leper would either be declared healed or not healed, clean or unclean.

Walking down the street, if the leper was asked, "How do you know you are healed?" The leper could boast with pride, and give this testimony, "Jesus healed me. I went to the priest, the priest examined me and said I was completely healed, so I no longer have to say unclean to every person who I come in contact with!"

If you, for any reason, think that God has healed your body, a visit to the doctor is quite possibly the great-est step of faith you can take. He will examine you, perhaps x-ray you, but regardless of the test he can pronounce you to be clean or unclean. Let the doctor decide whether or not you can flush the pills.

You will then be able to walk down the street and if someone says, "I hear you've been sick—how are you doing?" You can say, "Haven't you heard, I called for the elders of the church last week, and they came and prayed for me. I felt that God had healed my body, so I went to the doctor; he examined me, took x-rays and said I was fine. He took me off all the medication I was taking, and now I just can't stop praising God!"

Jesus knew exactly what He was doing when He said, "Go show yourself to the priest."

Now, it is time for you as a minister to attend confession.

What would you vote to be the single most dreaded part of your job, the part which drains you of so much your time, gets into your mind and consumes your concentration, robbing you of sleep at the midnight hour?

Most pastors give that distinct honor to the time spent counseling. People constantly want your advice about matters in their lives, which are without doubt, very important situations. They want you to make decisions for them. Never underestimate the compliment that a person gives you when they ask your advice. But then on the other hand, never take lightly the responsibility that rests on your shoulders to give good, sound, professional counsel.

If you are not careful you will find yourself spending hours upon hours listening to problems for which you have no answers. Maybe you're saying: "Isn't that part of your job?" Not really; perhaps we should listen as a courtesy, but in all truthfulness, in most areas, we are not qualified to give advice.

YOUR PASTOR NEEDS THIS BOOK

<u>Oh, now that hurt, didn't it</u>? We cannot give professional advice, just our personal opinions. It's true. If we are not qualified, we are really only offering our opinions.

In your office I'm sure you have a brag wall with every accolade ever bestowed on you. I had one; I filled it with plaques, awards, newspaper articles, anything I felt displayed my accomplishments. I am sure every degree you worked so hard for is mounted and displayed on your wall in the exact same way a hunter will mount his trophy deer head to silently preach to everyone who sees it, his qualifications. And rightfully so. You worked hard to quality yourself in certain areas of expertise, and you should display your credentials.

Every documented college and university degree you earned is probably displayed in a frame on that particular wall. The one from seminary you attended is probably there. Any licenses that qualify you for certain things probably hang on that wall.

Now, sit in your chair, <u>look at your wall</u> and be honest with yourself, according to your credentials. Are you, most of the time, offering counsel beyond your scope of training? In spite of your wall of documentation, the answer is probably a great big yes.

- Are you licensed to practice law?
- Are you licensed to give financial advice?
- Are you licensed to give marriage counseling?
- Are you licensed to discuss sexual problems?
- Are you licensed for drug rehabilitation?
- Are you licensed for medical advice?
- Are you licensed in child behavior?

Go, Show Yourself To The Priest

<u>Next question</u>, why do you do this, give advice in areas where you have no training?
<u>Next question</u>, is it eating up your time?
<u>Next question</u>, is it placing undue stress on you?
<u>Next question</u>, are you seeing any results?

What has God called and qualified and equipped you for? Whatever God has called you to do, that is the area where you should be exerting your energy. That is the area where you will produce fruit.

True, there should be many arms of the local church that reach out to the community, but that does not mean that God intended for you to be involved in every arm of ministry.

What were you called to do?

If you had to sum up your calling in one sentence, what would you write?
Fill in the blank: God called me to_____.

If you're going to survive in the ministry, you need to focus on what God has called you to do. That sounds easy, but it is not. The reason it is so difficult is because our religious community has loaded upon the shoulders of preachers, so much "stuff" that God has not called us to do. There can be tremendous peer pressure if the former pastor did all these things, or the pastor across town does them.

Add to that the fact that we as preachers have for so long led people to believe that we can do it all. Because we think it is expected of us, we make feeble attempts to be all things to all people. We were never called to wear many hats. God called us to be specialists. <u>You need to get a hold of that fact</u>.

The twelve disciples at Jerusalem had a decision to make; there was a legitimate problem that had arisen among the believers. Some of the immigrant widows were not being fed daily as the other widows were. It appears the early church took very seriously the commands in the Old Testament concerning the treatment of widows. See Deuteronomy 10:18; 14:29; 16:11, 14; 24:17, 19-21; and 26:12-13.

Acts 6:1-4 [NIV] In those days when the number of disciples was increasing, the Grecian Jews among them complained against the Hebraic Jews because their widows were being overlooked in the daily distribution of food. So the Twelve gathered all the disciples together and said, "It would not be right for us to neglect the ministry of the word of God in order to wait on tables. Brothers, choose seven men from among you who are known to be full of the Spirit and wisdom. We will turn this responsibility over to them and will give our attention to prayer and the ministry of the word."

This is how the disciples handled the situation; they looked at the calling on their lives, and then they looked at the problem involving the widows. They could have very easily said, "Don't worry about the widows. We will take them food every day." It was something that needed to be done daily, and it was expected of the church. They did not question the validity of the need. What weighed on the mind of the disciples was this; will the task in any way interfere with our primary responsibility?

After determining that waiting on the widows would indeed interfere with what they were called to do, which was to minister the Word and pray, the disciples appointed other men in the church to fill the position of ministering to the widows.

Then notice what happen immediately after the Apostles prayed and laid their hands on the men who were going to be involved in the daily distribution of food to the widows. The very next verse, verse 7, "So the word of God spread. The number of disciples in Jerusalem increased rapidly, and a large number of priests became obedient to the faith."

Because the disciples chose to pray and preach, rather than wait on tables, the number of disciples in Jerusalem increased rapidly.

Are you waiting tables more than fulfilling your office of minister of the gospel?

The bread that you, as a minister, are supposed to be delivering is the bread that will cause people to never hunger again. It is called the bread of life.

Jesus said in John 6:48 [NIV] "I am the bread of life. Your forefathers ate the manna in the desert, yet they died. But here is the bread that comes down from heaven, which a man may eat and not die. I am the living bread that came down from heaven. If anyone eats of this bread, he will live forever. This bread is my flesh, which I will give for the life of the world."

In the same way, Moses found himself in a very stressful situation, in Exodus 18. Remember, Moses was eighty plus years old when he led Israel in the wilderness. Moses was smart enough to leave his family, his wife and two sons, with his father-in-law when he went into Egypt to confront Pharaoh.

In this chapter Moses' father-in-law, Jethro, brought Moses' family to him in the wilderness. It is note-worthy that Jethro is not an Israelite; neither is he a believer in the one true God that Moses believed in. Together they celebrated all that God had done for Moses and the Children of Israel. Jethro even offered a burnt offering and other sacrifices to God. Aaron and the elders of Israel ate bread with Jethro. It was a joyful occasion--their family reunion, and everyone was happy.

The next day, after the family reunion, the son-in-law had to go back to work.

Exodus 18:13 [NIV] "The next day Moses took his seat to serve as judge for the people, and they stood around him from morning till evening."

His father-in-law decided to drop by the office to see what his son-in-law was working on. When Jethro saw what Moses was doing, he simply could not believe his eyes.

In Exodus 18:14 [NIV] we see Jethro's response. "What is this you are doing for the people? Why do you alone sit as judge, while all these people stand around you from morning till evening?"

There is no doubt that Moses was a great man; the Bible says he was the most humble man on earth, but his pastoring skills left much to be desired. Moses was trying to do it all, all alone. As a result, everyone was suffering. Moses was killing himself and the people had to wait and wait and wait for help.

What amazes me about this passage of scripture is the fact that it took an outside voice to offer a solution. If Moses could not see the problem it seems like someone in Israel would have. But they didn't. It took Jethro, an outsider and someone close to Moses, to identify the problem and offer a solution.

In effect, Jethro took Moses aside and pointed out his job description. Exodus 18:20 says, "Teach them the decrees and laws, and show them the way to live and the duties they are to perform."

Go, Show Yourself To The Priest

And that means for all the other "stuff", he had to find capable men.

Let me boil this down; look on your wall, to find what you are qualified to do. Focus only on that. For all the other "stuff", refer your congregation to a Christian in that field who is qualified to give counsel. You should make it your business to meet Christian professional people to whom you would feel good about referring your congregation.

- Get to know a Bible-believing M.D.
- Search until you find a God-fearing attorney.
- Search your city for a qualified Christian marriage counselor
- Locate a trustworthy Christian financial advisor.
- Find a Christian drug treatment facility.

When sincere people come to you looking for answers to perplexing problems in their lives, be ready and willing to pray with them about their problems, and then point them to qualified help. The harsh truth is that your parishioners can have very personal problems in their lives that you are better off not knowing.

I personally know a guy who, at one time, was a very good pastor. But then he grew cold and backslid while pastoring a church, he was totally burned out. Ultimately he should have never listened to a nice young lady's personal problems, he was not qualified.

YOUR PASTOR NEEDS THIS BOOK

This chapter in a nut-shell:

God has called you to preach the good news, so learn to refer your congregation to Christian professionals for counseling in areas in which you are not trained.

Appendix 1

Scripture quotations.